ESSAYS ON BLACK LITERATURES

CONNECTIONS

ESSAYS ON BLACK LITERATURES

CONNECTIONS

EDITED BY

EMMANUEL S NELSON

 ABORIGINAL STUDIES PRESS   CANBERRA 1988

First published in 1988 by
Aboriginal Studies Press
for the Australian Institute of Aboriginal Studies
GPO Box 553, Canberra, ACT 2601.

The views expressed in this publication are those of the authors and not necessarily those of the Australian Institute of Aboriginal Studies.

National Library of Australia Cataloguing-in-Publication data:

Connections: essays on Black literatures.

Includes bibliographies.
ISBN 0 85575 186 X.

1. Literature—Black authors. [2]. Australian literature—Aboriginal authors. I. Nelson, Emmanuel S. (Emmanuel Sampath), 1954- .
II. Australian Institute of Aboriginal Studies. III. Conference on Black Literatures (1986: University of Queensland).

809'.8896

Cover designed by Em Squared.

Typeset in Compugraphic Century Schoolbook by Aboriginal Studies Press.

Printed in Australia by Australian Print Group.

3000 01 88

Contents

Contributors

Arlene A Elder is an Associate Professor of English and Comparative Literature at the University of Cincinnati. Dr Elder, who received her PhD from the University of Chicago, was a Visiting Fulbright Professor at the University of Nairobi in 1976. Author of *'The Hindered Hand': Cultural Implications of Early African-American Fiction* (1978), she is currently finishing a comparative study of African and Afro-American dramatists and is beginning work on the plays of Jack Davis.

David Headon lectures at University College, University of New South Wales (Australian Defence Force Academy). His main areas of research interest are Australian/Aboriginal literatures and nineteenth century American writing. Author of recent articles on John Lang, Daniel Deniehy and David Campbell, he is currently collecting material for an anthology of Northern Territory literature to be published in 1988.

Theodore R Hudson is a Graduate Professor of English at Howard University, Washington, DC. In addition to numerous scholarly articles, he has published *From Leroi Jones to Amiri Baraka: The Literary Works* (1974) which won the College Language Association's award for distinguished literary scholarship. Dr Hudson is currently engaged in a study of Edward 'Duke' Ellington as a music–literature synaesthesian.

Trevor James received his PhD in English from the University of London and is currently Senior Lecturer in English at the Darwin Institute of Technology. In addition to numerous articles on Commonwealth literatures, he has authored two books: *English Literature From the Third World* (Longman, 1986) and *The Metraphysical Poets* (Longman, 1987). He is currently writing a handbook of Australian literature and compiling an anthology of Aboriginal literature.

Daniel Kunene is an internationally known scholar in African Studies, and a South African by birth. A Professor of African languages and literatures at the University of Wisconsin at Madison, he has authored several books and scholarly articles. He is currently a Visiting Scholar at the Institute for Ethnology and African Studies at Johannes Gutenberg University in West Germany.

Stephen Muecke   teaches writing and textual theory at the New South Wales Institute of Technology. He has published *Gularabulu* (with Paddy Roe, 1983) and *Reading the Country* (with Roe and Benterrak, 1984), and has published in the areas of semiotics, discourse theory and Aboriginal literature.

Emmanuel S Nelson   received his undergraduate education in India and his MA and PhD from the University of Tennessee. A specialist in Afro-American literature, he has held Visiting Assistant Professorships at Colby College (Maine) and at York College (CUNY). During 1985–86 he was a Postdoctoral Research Fellow at the University of Queensland and currently is an Assistant Professor of Afro-American and Third World literatures at the State University College of New York at Cortland. He has published several articles on ethnic American and Aboriginal Australian literatures.

Adam Shoemaker   holds a PhD in English from the Australian National University, Canberra. His doctoral thesis, titled 'Black Words, White Page: The Nature and History of Aboriginal Literature, 1929–84' will be published in revised form in 1988. Currently, Dr Shoemaker is co-editing with Jack Davis and Stephen Muecke the first national anthology of Aboriginal writing.

Roberta B Sykes   is a Queenslander who holds a PhD from Harvard University. A leading black Australian intellectual, she has been and continues to be an outspoken civil rights activist. Author of *Incentive, Achievement and Community: An Analysis of Black Viewpoints on Issues Relating to Black Australian Education* (George Allen and Unwin, 1986), she is currently a consultant to the National Bureau of Crime Statistics and Research, Sydney.

Cliff Watego   holds an MA in English from the University of Queensland. A prominent black Australian scholar, he has published articles on Aboriginal as well as South Pacific literatures. He lives in Brisbane and plans to pursue doctoral study in black literary theory. In 1987 he received a modest grant from the Australia Council's Aboriginal Arts Board to prepare his MA thesis, 'Identity and Politics in Contemporary Aboriginal Literature', for publication.

Acknowledgments

All papers in this anthology were initially presented at the Conference on Black Literatures—an event that was made possible by the active support and cooperation of many individuals and organisations. I wish to extend special thanks to Cliff Watego, my co-convener, without whose help the conference could not have become a reality. My colleagues at the University of Queensland—Jeanie Bell, Ken Goodwin, Bernard Minol, Chris Tiffin and Helen Tiffin—worked tirelessly and they made the conference a huge success. Ron Marks and Peter Edwards of the University of Queensland, through moral and material support, encouraged and inspired everyone involved in organising the event. Further, I would like to acknowledge the generous financial support offered by the following bodies—University of Queensland, Aboriginal Arts Board of the Australia Council, Australian Department of Foreign Affairs, Government of Papua New Guinea, Literature Board of the Australia Council, and the United States Information Agency.

Introduction

Emmanuel S Nelson

At least in a limited academic sense, the Conference on Black Literatures held at the University of Queensland in June 1986 was an historical occasion. Conferences that address issues in black literatures, of course, are not new; what made the Brisbane conference a unique event was its location and its content. It was the first international conference of its kind to be held in Australia; and it was the first conference, anywhere in the world, to place Australian Aboriginal and South Pacific literatures along with other conventionally black literatures of the African Diaspora.

The Australian location was significant. Had the conference been held in the United States, in the Caribbean or in Africa, the focus, inevitably, would have been on the black literatures of the Diaspora. The Australian venue, therefore, made it easy for the conveners to decentre those black literary traditions and to highlight Aboriginal and South Pacific writing. Such a strategy proved effective in countering the marginality of indigenous Australian and South Pacific literatures on international forums. It also encouraged the delegates—especially those scholars from Africa, the Afro-Caribbean and Afro-American—to confront and to examine the black experience in this part of the world. It was, to many, a new revelation.

Even more significant than the location was the content of the conference. By placing Aboriginal and South Pacific literatures along with the literatures of the African Diaspora under the broad rubric of black literatures, the conference offered a fundamental challenge to the received notions of the term 'black'. The word black, which became fashionable among Afro-Americans during the sixties, was popularised by the Black Power rhetoric of racial self-affirmation and cultural assertiveness. It was a word that had traditionally carried a cluster of negative connotations in the Western context; but the word was redeemed and made wholesome through a supreme act of cultural and linguistic reappropriation. The notion of blackness became a renewed version of the earlier Negritude. Soul became a symbolic essence of modern black consciousness. The word, however, was used generally in an Afro-American context. The Black Studies programmes that proliferated on American campuses during the sixties focused mostly on the Afro-American component of the black experience. Even the African and Afro-Caribbean aspects remained largely marginalised. Black literature generally meant black American literature. The word black thus became almost an Afro-American cultural and political monopoly. When it was used in a broader sense—as Amiri Baraka (*Black Magic*), Bonnie Barthold (*Black*

Time), Henry Louis Gates (*Black Literature and Literary Theory*) and others have done—it referred only to the peoples of the African Diaspora. The scope was strictly trans-Atlantic. But the conference in Brisbane insisted on making the term less exclusive by focusing on the black experience in Australia and the South Pacific. The conference, especially through panel discussions, encouraged scholarly exploration of the theoretical and methodological implications of taking blackness beyond the boundaries of the African Diaspora. The purpose of the conference was not to endorse but to challenge; the declared goal was not to preserve but to disrupt.

In this the conference was eminently successful. One of the distinguished delegates, Professor Ron Baxter Miller of the University of Tennessee, while cautioning that the black experience was not a monolith, spoke of 'common structures' among various black experiences. Another prominent participant, Professor Theodore Hudson, commented on 'parallels' between black literatures of the South Pacific and those of the African Diaspora. He went on to point out that there was a 'universality' in the way in which people write about oppression. Professor Lemuel Johnson of the University of Michigan, a leading scholar in African literary studies, declared that the term 'Aboriginality' can indeed be used as a general term to discuss the experiences and literature of all black peoples of the world.

Others began to call for redefinitions and new concepts. It became obvious from the enthusiasm and excitement of the conference participants—many of whom are key figures in Black Studies programmes in the United States—that the orthodox notions of blackness can no longer be held on to comfortably. Scholars in the field can no longer justify provincial and exclusive definitions of blackness. They no longer can conveniently ignore black Australian and black South Pacific literatures, since they can no longer claim ignorance of the existence of such literatures. Australian scholars who study Aboriginal and South Pacific writing, too, can no longer overlook the connections between these and other black literatures. Comparative approaches to and global perspectives on black writing in this part of the world are now inevitable.

Ripple effects of the conference are already evident. Papers on Aboriginal and South Pacific literatures were given at the 1987 Convention of the Modern Language Association. Professor Arlene Elder of the University of Cincinnati, who has in the past done excellent comparative studies of the African Diaspora literatures has now embarked on a study of Jack Davis's plays. She also organised a special session on Aboriginal literature at the 1987 national meeting of the United States based African Literature Association (ALA); this is the first time such a session was a part of the ALA's programme. The participants in the session included Professors Lemuel Johnson, Neville Choonoo and myself—all alumni of the Conference on Black Literatures in Brisbane! It appears certain that Aboriginal and South Pacific literatures will now become a permanent feature of black literary forums in the United States and elsewhere.

Any critical approach that seeks to study various literatures in a comparative framework should also be conscious of the vital differences among those literatures and among the cultures that create them. Our perception of similarities should not weaken our awareness of differences. Vast historical, political, linguistic and cultural differences do exist among various black peoples and these differences do shape their literary traditions. The historical experiences of various black groups, for example, differ widely. The Africans and the indigenous peoples of the South Pacific were defeated and colonised on their own land; blacks in the New World, however, are descendants of Africans who were not only colonised but also forcibly transported to alien and hostile lands. The psychological and cultural implications of these experiential differences are enormous.

The contemporary conditions of various black groups differ as well. Many African, South Pacific and Caribbean peoples now live in independent countries in which they constitute the dominant power groups; black Australians and black Americans, on the contrary, are denigrated minority groups in predominantly white countries. (It should be noted, however, that black Americans, in contrast to black Australians, are a much larger minority group and they are also, in relative terms, vastly more powerful—economically, politically and culturally.)

There are ethnic differences too. While the African, Afro-Caribbean and Afro-American peoples share a common racial origin, they are ethnically unrelated to the indigenous peoples of the South Pacific and Australia. Language is yet another source of difference. Unlike Afro-American and Aboriginal writers, many African and South Pacific writers choose to create imaginative literature in a language to which they are not native. There is, therefore, an ongoing, frequently creative, tension between the reality implied in the imported imperial language and the reality apprehended by them in their indigenous languages. And while all black written literatures have relatively brief traditions—in contrast to, say, the literature of India or Iran or Greece—some are more recent than others. Afro-American writing, for example, is more than two hundred years old; in contrast, the Papua New Guinea writing began less than two decades ago, with the launching of the literary magazine *Kovave* in 1968.

What, then, warrants a comparative study of the literatures of these diverse black cultures? The most obvious attribute all black peoples share, of course, is their colonial past. Some of them, black South Africans for example, still remain colonised; many Caribbean island-nations remain locked into a paracolonial relationship with the United States; and even the independent African and South Pacific nations continue to face varying degrees of neocolonial economic, political and cultural pressures. So there emerges a pattern of defeat, dispossession and denigration in the historical character of all black experiences. This common colonial heritage and the debilitating psychological and cultural consequences link, in a fundamental way, the diverse black experiences around the world. The literatures that articulate those experiences, therefore, are comparable.

This common historical inheritance accounts for a variety of similarities among various black literatures. The visions of all black writers are characterised by what WEB Dubois, one of the greatest black intellectuals of the modern era, referred to as 'double consciousness' and what Peter Bruck has characterised more recently as 'bicultural ambivalence'. A vibrant tradition of protest is common to all black literatures. Black texts frequently share a complex relationship with Western texts. Perhaps because of subtle connections between political powerlessness and autobiographical impulse, there is a preponderance of autobiographical narratives in most black literary traditions. There are thematic similarities too: searching for cultural wholeness, forging a healing and liberating sense of self, seeking strength in community, reconstructing the past, subverting white texts, recreating rituals and ceremonies, celebrating blackness. Black writers share many problems as well: reconciling their artistic and political responsibilities; containing their black realities in a Western linguistic medium; articulating their non-European sensibilities through largely European aesthetic forms; managing the complex demands and expectations of their audiences.

There are, then, certain common resonances among various black literatures and these, I believe, justify a broad comparative approach. The political connections, spiritual affinities and historical similarities indeed invite comparative investigations. These links, which are engendered by shared dispossession and colonial dislocation, form the basis of an aesthetics of resistance. It is this perception of a shared aesthetics—which shapes the themes and structures of black literary traditions everywhere—that prompted the ambitious conference at the University of Queensland.

All eight essays in this anthology were first read at the conference. Four of them discuss Aboriginal writing; one is a comparative study of Afro-American, Aboriginal and Maori literatures; one deals with black South African writing; and two discuss black American literature. The Aboriginal focus of the volume is deliberate; this work is intended largely as an exploration and assessment of black Australian writing in the international context of other black literatures. But all essays raise issues that point to basic connections among these literatures and indicate areas in which the concerns of individual traditions intersect with those of other black traditions.

Cliff Watego's 'Backgrounds to Aboriginal Literature' provides an excellent overview of the development of black literature in Australia—from the works of David Unaipon in the 1920s to the major contributions of contemporary writers, such as Kath Walker, Jack Davis, Colin Johnson, Archie Weller and Gerry Bostock. Watego's discussion of Aboriginal writing raises a number of issues that are relevant to other black literatures as well. For example, the close connection that Watego perceives between Aboriginal political activism and Aboriginal imaginative literature exists in all black literary traditions. (Theodore Hudson's chapter cogently establishes a similar connection in Afro-American writing.) Historically for black writers everywhere the art of writing has also been a political enterprise, a revolutionary act of resistance. Black literatures and black revolutions move together; one reinforces and sustains the other. If black writers are the public sounds of their community weeping, as Roberta Sykes argued in her keynote address to the conference, then it is not difficult to understand why many black creative writers are also passionate political activists.

Watego's sensitive discussion of David Unaipon's difficult role as the first Aboriginal writer again reminds one of comparable difficulties that early black writers had to contend with in the United States. Unaipon 'christianised' Aboriginal legends in order to reach a white audience. Phillis Wheatley, America's first black female poet, sometimes pandered to white prejudices simply to be heard. She had to mute the tone of her protest in order to be published. Her need, like Unaipon's, to find an audience encouraged her sometimes to compromise her fidelity to the realities of black experience.

The political–literary paradigm that Watego establishes to explore the development of Aboriginal writing, again, has validity in the Afro-American, Afro-Caribbean and African contexts. Unaipon's protest is tentative; the revolt of Bostock and Gilbert is uncompromisingly aggressive; but the most recent Aboriginal writing, as Cliff Watego points out, is not so much concerned with protesting white atrocities (though such protest was earlier seen as necessary to define Aboriginal identity) but with regenerating the black self. There is a gradual movement away from protest toward sophisticated cultural self-criticism. A similar themative shift is also discernible in African and Afro-Caribbean literatures: from the nationalistic defiance of pre-Independence writing to the increasingly self-critical concerns of the postcolonial condition. (The shift in Chinua Achebe's perspective from his first novel *Things Fall Apart* to his recent non-fiction *The Trouble With Nigeria* is a classic example of this movement.) A comparable development appears in Afro-American writing as well. The protest tradition, which reached its militant climax during the sixties, is giving way to less strident writing. The recent works of Toni Morrison, Alice Walker, John Wideman and many others are not as engaged in protest as they are in exploring all dimensions of the Afro-American experience.

David Headon's '"The Coming of the Dingoes": Black/White Interaction in the Literature of the Northern Territory', with its excellent bibliographic information, argues that it is not yet possible 'to piece together a coherent history based on Aboriginal oral, and written, testimony'. The existing material can still 'act as an appropriate and damning corrective to the scores of white fiction and non-fiction accounts' of Australia's frontier. The Aboriginal past can now be redeemed, since the story of Australia can now be told from an Aboriginal perspective. These oral and written testimonies—

and the historical novels of Faith Bandler and Colin Johnson—subvert colonialist historical discourses and rescue black Australian past from distortion and dismissal. This reappropriation of the past, of course, is vital to heal the trauma of postcontact dislocation and to regain a sense of personal and collective wholeness. These imaginative reconstructions of history provide redemptive visions of the past, visions that can be spiritually cleansing and self-affirming. This rewriting of history, again, is an attribute that black Australian writing shares with other black literatures. Achebe's *Things Fall Apart* recovers Ibo past, as Johnson's *Doctor Wooreddy's Prescription for Enduring the Ending of the World* reappropriates Aboriginal past; both are imaginative attempts to heal the cultural fracture caused by the catastrophic impact of colonial intervention. Similarly, Bandler's *Wacvie* is a black Australian counterpart of the Afro-American *Roots*, though the latter work is a much larger one with an epic sweep.

Stephen Muecke's 'Body, Inscription, Epistemology: Knowing Aboriginal Texts' addresses the complex cultural, political and linguistic difficulties involved in 'translating' traditional Aboriginal verbal art into written texts. The transformation 'from body to book' entails violence to the original form by destroying 'the aesthetic or performative dimension'; yet, production of 'a written text which is more than performed speech' (as Muecke's and Paddy Roe's *Gularabulu*) tends to ignore the vast 'traditional knowledge which historically precedes such production'. Muecke examines the problem, drawing from his own experience and expertise in textual transformation and from postmodernist theories of literary production.

The concerns that Muecke articulates are also at the centre of Daniel Kunene's '*Ingqumbo/The Wrath*: An Analysis of a Translation'. Using AC Jordan's self-translation of his Xhosa novel (*Ingqumbo*) into English (*The Wrath*), Kunene, like Muecke, explores the complicated cultural, political and linguistic problems in translation. The issues Kunene addresses in the black South African context have compelling significance in the black Australian context as well. Kunene, for example, points out that 'there are intangibles in the language which cannot be quantified or objectified as lexical items'. How much inevitable violence, then, does a scribe, even an informed scribe, inflict on the Aboriginal oral text when she or he attempts to translate it into a written text? Kunene also demonstrates how AC Jordan's awareness of a non-Xhosa, potentially hostile, audience for his *The Wrath* affected his translation of the original version written in Xhosa for an understanding Xhosa audience.

This question of audience also has relevance in the translation of Aboriginal verbal art. The communicative context itself, in which an Aboriginal narrator speaks to a non-Aboriginal narratee, can determine meanings. If so, it appears that one can voice legitimate concerns regarding the accuracy of the narrative itself. Yet another observation made by Kunene points to a comparable problem facing translators of Aboriginal oral texts: the translator might understand lexical items superficially but might fail to grasp 'deeper cultural codings'. Aboriginal English, like black English in the United States, is a complex language with its own grammatical patterns; it has its own cultural codes, semantic levels and subversive strategies that a non-Aboriginal listener or reader might fail to comprehend correctly. Can a non-Aboriginal narratee, then, fully enter the semantic field of the narrator?

If the issues that Kunene raises regarding translation are relevant in the Aboriginal context, so are his suggestions. He argues that in the act of translation, at least ideally, concern for propriety should transcend that of proprietorship; that loyalty to the original work is indispensable; that a high level of linguistic competence is essential; and that the translator should not only be bilingual but should be functionally bicultural as well.

Adam Shoemaker's paper on Colin Johnson, Jack Davis and Archie Weller examines the most neglected area in Aboriginal writing—the short story. He points out that the first volume of short stories by a black Australian was published only in 1986 and he attributes the relative paucity of black short fiction in Australia to two factors: one, writers find poetry and drama to be more powerful vehicles for expressing their political aspirations; two, the economics of the literary marketplace makes short fiction a less viable commercial proposition. It is interesting to note a similar pattern, for similar reasons, in the development of Afro-American short stories.

Paul Lawrence Dunbar's *Folks From Dixie*, the first anthology of short stories by a black American, was published in 1898—more than one hundred years after the publication of Phillis Wheatley's poetry. And just as the now defunct *Identity* offered aspiring Aboriginal writers, who were largely denied access to white-owned periodicals, to publish short stories, black American writers of short fiction, too, were able to find a forum only when black-owned periodicals, such as *The Crisis* (1910) and *Opportunity* (1923), were founded. A similar trend is noticeable in black South Africa as well, although the rest of Africa has a much more prolific tradition in short fiction. Despite the fact that Peter Abrahams, a South African, was the first black writer on the continent to publish an anthology of short stories (*Dark Testament*, 1942), this literary form grew substantially only in the sixties and seventies, only when largely black-run journals, such as *Drum* and *Zonk*, were established.

Trevor James in his 'Black Literatures in the South Pacific: The Spider and the Bee' takes a comparative approach to Afro-American, Aboriginal and Maori literatures. Through an ingenious application of the Swiftian metaphor of the spider and the bee, he examines the development patterns of these literary traditions. Black American writers, he points out, have successfully handled the initial 'physical absence of a cultural base', caused by forced displacement from home, by creating a strong and viable one in the new land. Maori writers, on the other hand, have been sustained by their cultural base which, despite the disruption and damage caused by the colonial intervention, has been kept in tact to a considerable extent. James argues that Aboriginal writers, in contrast to black American and Maori writers, do not have a potent cultural base to speak from. The colonial assault was so devastating that the Aboriginal culture still remains deeply traumatised. If James's assessment is right, the tasks and the responsibilities that face contemporary and future Aboriginal writers are indeed enormous.

Theodore Hudson's 'Activism and Criticism During the Black Arts Movement' cogently explores the close connections between art and politics in black America during the revolutionary sixties. As examples of 'direct links between community activism and literary criticism', Hudson points to the dramatic increase in the number of black periodicals during the sixties, establishment of several black-owned publishing companies and creation of Black Studies programmes in practically every major American university. Perhaps the most significant connection between activism and art during the sixties lies in the formulation of the Black Aesthetic which proposed 'a radical reordering of the western cultural aesthetic...a separate symbolism, mythology, critique, and iconology'. It argued that black art should be collective, functional and committed. It called for an intellectual 'assault against the restrictive assumptions of the white critics'. Although Hudson's discussion is limited to the black American context, it has broad relevance to literary theory and critical practice in other black contexts as well.

African cultural nationalists, such as Chinweizu, Onwucheckwa Jemie, Ihechukwu Madubuke and others, have sought to liberate African literature and literary criticism from the European-colonialist aesthetic. Among notable Afro-Caribbean writers and critics who have voiced similar concerns are Edward Brathwaite and Michael Thelwell. Calls for a Black Aesthetic are heard in Australia too. Cliff Watego has chastised the intellectually limited and culturally insensitive assessment of black Australian literature by some white critics. Bruce McGuinness has called for 'community control' of black literary production and distribution. Denis Walker, at the 1983 Aboriginal Writers' Conference in Perth, denounced the application of European literary criteria to evaluations of Aboriginal art. At the same conference, Colin Johnson argued that Aboriginal writing should not be compared to white Australian literature. This resistance to Western aesthetic imperialism and attempts to decolonise literary criticism constitute yet another shared black intellectual concern.

Arlene Elder's 'Ed Bullins: Black Theatre as Ritual' examines the use and significance of ritual in contemporary Afro-American theatre, with special focus on the plays of Ed Bullins's ongoing Twentieth Century Cycle. Elder argues that Bullins's plays reveal his 'conscious return to the elements of traditional African oral performance and African-American folk roots' and his 'ability to couch revolutionary interpretations of the black American experience in ritual form, drawing on the traditions of black oratory, narrative, street talk, mythology, and, especially, music'. Bullins recognises the culturally regenerative and spiritually reaffirming potential of rituals that reinforce ancestral affinities by stressing a shared ontological sense. By infusing rituals into the dramatic mode, Bullins seeks to recreate 'the black spirit and African identity', thus providing his political theatre with a timeless dimension. In this respect, the plays of Jack Davis show a marked similarity to those of Ed Bullins. In *Kullark*, for example, dance, song and music are integral to its theme and structure. Like Bullins, Davis consciously incorporates rituals and ceremonies to assert the 'significance of an Aboriginality which cannot and should not be cast aside'.

The final essay in this anthology (see Appendix) is what was Roberta Sykes's keynote address to the conference. The theme of her speech is black unity; she calls for meaningful connections and alliances among all black peoples of the world. A global consolidation of the economic, political and cultural powers of black peoples, she argues, is vital for our survival. Her speech initiated a creative dialogue among the various black peoples at the conference. The purpose of this anthology is to keep that dialogue alive.

References

Abrahams, P.
1942 *Dark Testament*, Allen and Unwin, London.

Achebe, C.
1959 *Things Fall Apart*, Heinemann, London.

Bandler, F.
1977 *Wacvie*, Rigby, Adelaide.

Baraka, A.
1969 *Black Magic*, Bobbs-Merill, New York.

Barthold, B.
1981 *Black Time*, Yale University Press, New Haven.

Davis, J.
1978 *Kullark*, Currency Press, Sydney.

Davis, J. and Hodge, B. (eds)
1985 *Aboriginal Writing Today*, Australian Institute of Aboriginal Studies, Canberra.

Dunbar, P.L.
1898 *Folks From Dixie*, Ayer Publishers, New York.

Gates, H.L.
1984 *Black Literature and Literary Theory*, Methuen, New York.

Haley, A.
1976 *Roots*, Doubleday, New York.

Johnson, C.
1983 *Doctor Wooreddy's Prescription for Enduring the Ending of the World*, Hyland House, Melbourne.

Jordan, A.C.
1940 *Ingqumbo Yeminyanya*, The Lovedale Press, Lovedale.
1980 *The Wrath of the Ancestors*, The Lovedale Press, Lovedale.

Roe, P.
1983 *Gularabulu: Stories from the West Kimberley*, Fremantle Arts Centre Press, Fremantle.

Backgrounds to Aboriginal Literature

Cliff Watego

In February 1983 at the launching of Jack Davis's book of plays, *Kullark/The Dreamers*, the author spoke of how in the 1960s there was consensus among leading black activists to enlighten the white public to the grievances and aims of black Australians through literature. Davis explained that:

> We used to speak in those days when we were talking about politics—black politics—of how we were ₃oing to make ourselves heard within the white Australian society. And even in those days when we went back to our little dingy rooms, we said (referring to, among others, Kath Walker, Faith Bandler, and Ken Colbung), 'Well we've got to write about this, we've got to tell the people'.

The record sales of Kath Walker's first volume of poetry, *We Are Going* in 1964, was followed almost two years later by her second volume, *The Dawn is at Hand* which also sold extremely well. Together the sales ranked her among the highest-selling poets in Australian history and therefore set a promising example for other black writers to follow. No one could doubt that the poetry was already fulfilling the task of taking the Aboriginal side of the story into the homes of white Australia. In spite of the negative criticism of Walker's works by some white critics, the overall reception meant that there had emerged an audience conscious of the Aboriginal voice. This was encouraging from Davis's viewpoint. Davis (1970, vi) tells how he had flirted with verse since the 1930s when he 'became interested in writing as a means of expression'. He started writing more seriously in the postwar years, but never pursued publication. The significant fact is that involvement in the Aboriginal movement was the catalyst for both Walker and Davis to create an Aboriginal literary perspective, a perspective that would be sustained predominantly by the developing political situation.

In Davis's first volume, *The First Born and Other Poems* (1970), there are some poems which deal with themes not specifically Aboriginal in nature. But these were the exception rather than the norm to what had been a recognisable trend in Aboriginal poetry. Interestingly, most of Walker's unpublished poetry is distinctly detached from the Aboriginal movement. It was only after 1970, when she decided to quit the movement—a decision marked by her move to 'Moongalba' on North Stradbroke Island—that her published poetry branched into other areas. However, these few poems, most of which concerned either travel experiences or nature and conservation, were still balanced by poems devoted to the Aboriginal cause. There was, then, no substantial or lasting shift in the major preoccupation of her poetry. Thus Davis's contribution to Aboriginal poetry in 1970, through a mood and an expression which were strongly identifiable with those engendered in Walker's earlier works, helped to foster an indigenous, protest, literary tradition.

Further momentum was lent to this budding literature with the publication of Kevin Gilbert's *End of Dreamtime* (1971). This volume of poetry had undergone drastic editing. Nonetheless, the printing of the book was a major achievement, given the extraordinary circumstances hindering the overall process. (Kevin Gilbert was in gaol at the time, serving the last couple of years of a fourteen year prison term.) Yet despite these factors, his major themes, tone and temper survived to reinforce the perspective of Walker and Davis. *End of Dreamtime* bristles with celebrations of Aboriginality and denunciations of white Australia for its maltreatment of Aborigines. The impetus given to the Aboriginal literary field by Gilbert also extended into the forum of political activism. Walker and Davis were both in the vanguard of the efforts of the Federal Council for the Advancement of Aborigines and Torres Strait Islanders (FCAATSI) which spearheaded the Aboriginal movement throughout the 1960s. It was not long after his release from prison that Gilbert also displayed an acumen for political enterprise. This manifested itself in an original attempt to draw broad attention to the Aboriginal cause. This was through the peaceful demonstration that became known as the Aboriginal 'Tent Embassy' erected on Australia Day 1972. As Gilbert (1984, 3) says:

> In 1972, when (Prime Minister) McMahon brought down his land denial policy, stating his government would only consider short term leases...not ownership for Aborigines and their land, I gathered together five young Aborigines from Redfern and we decided we must act more directly and erect a permanent camp outside Parliament House.

Although it may have seemed a novel attraction to the great number of sightseers that visited Australia's capital, the Embassy, just like Aboriginal poetry which also undoubtedly attracted its share of curious readers, was successful in gaining attention, both local and overseas, to the Aboriginal plight. But the importance of this incident from a literary standpoint lay in the fact that it was a hallmark of Aboriginal protest which inspired a long poem by Gerry Bostock, who would become another major figure in Aboriginal writing.

Bostock was actively involved in the Tent Embassy demonstration that lasted until July 1972, when its forced abandonment sparked violent scenes. The Embassy was destined to become a modern, purely black Australian (as distinct from imported) symbol of land rights, freedom and injustice. Bostock's (1980, 14–18) most widely-read poem 'Black Children', mirrors the black nationalistic pride with which Aborigines, then and since, have embraced these ideals to carry the movement forward. It is a movement which the federal and state governments had threatened to sink into the growing disillusionment that had become more than apparent since the 1967 referendum. The overwhelming vote in the referendum to allow blacks to be counted as citizens and to give the federal government power to legislate for all blacks had given the Aboriginal community and its supporters cause for optimism. But in the following four years it became clear that the federal government was not prepared to use such powers of legislature to improve matters. The black movement, in particular that body of consciousness-raising blacks, felt it had been betrayed. The black community had waited in anticipation for the government policies aimed at self-determination for blacks to unfold. Black spokespersons (predominantly FCAATSI members) had continually reiterated that their people were not only ready but eager to prove to white society that they could manage their own affairs.

The period after 1967 was one of frustrated waiting, aggravated by setbacks such as the delaying of the Gurindji land claim and the disillusioning Gove land rights decision in 1971. From the Aboriginal viewpoint, Prime Minister McMahon's statement was a flat denial of land rights. It reaffirmed the patronising attitude of a government which, tongue-in-cheek, advocated self-determination. In a poem that predates the McMahon decision by at least two years, Gilbert (1971, 25) fired a rallying cry to his people to 'Stand up and be counted' or 'see our last hopes die'. But these were not prophetic insights. Gilbert's warnings reflected a mood of restrained anger which would vent itself in the prolonged stance of the Aboriginal Embassy.

As a symbol of land rights, the Embassy was also a symbol of survival against what was seen as the white man's most recent attempt to nullify Aborigines. The racial tension over land rights had been inflamed the previous year through the tour of the South African Springboks Rugby team. By condoning this tour, the Australian government was testifying to its own paternalistic attitude toward blacks in this country. Eradicating the indigenes' affinity with the land—either through judicial procedure or government policy—was a more subtle form of genocide. Gerry Bostock (1980, 14) implored his race, 'Rise up black children'. He repeated the urgent need to rebel against a patronage that infests the minds of whites, and to throw off the self-deceit which had been instilled in blacks by the 'white Judas brother'.

Although betrayal is a common theme for Aboriginal writers, the Judas symbol was used by Bostock to magnify the subtlety with which forces were, and still are, acting upon Aborigines at all levels to deprive them of their heritage, and consequently their future. When Gilbert (1978, 46) earlier addressed himself to the Gurindji campaigners he told them that their protest of silent fasting was 'A moment's irritation/Or idle curiosity' to white society, rather than a thorn in its conscience. He implied that white apathy would not allow their demonstration to amount to anything more than this. Bostock's 'Black Children' (1980, 17) is more explicit:

> Society has cast you aside
> And you've been made to hide

And grovel in the gutter,
And all you've done is to sit and mope
And mutter
About life without hope.

Bridging the thoughts of both poets is the notion that passivity is not only something expected in Aborigines by their oppressors but, moreover, the oppressor is contemptuous of such inaction. It is a condition typical of the master–slave relationship, in which the master expects the subordinate to be servile and obedient. But because the underling lacks the will or the power to initiate actions, he/she is despised. Gilbert (1978, 46) articulates this greater paradox facing the silent oppressed in his poem titled 'The Gurindji':

Justice, deprived of a strong voice slowly
Inexorably dies
And the seeker of justice dies with it
Or silently becomes a slave.

With his/her finger on the pulse of the black community's mood the Aboriginal writer had ensured that the Aboriginal voice remained strong in the search for justice. A decade had elapsed since Kath Walker first presented her poem 'Aboriginal Charter of Rights' at a FCAATSI meeting in Adelaide in 1962. After reciting this poeticised, Aboriginal version of *The United Nations Declaration of Human Rights* she recalled that the audience sat silent. She had spoken, for instance, of freedom 'from a bureaucrat Protection', 'incentive not restriction', 'self-reliance', and equal opportunity as equal human beings. The silence may well have been due to the dual factors that the speaker was not only an Aborigine, but also a woman. The response, however, indicated that foremost in the minds of the Aboriginal delegates in the audience was that here was one of their people espousing the principles and ideals that lay closest to the consciousness of the black communities they represented. In her own words Kath Walker (Schwenke 1977) recalls, 'Then every black man and woman was on their feet saying, "I want a copy". And I was frightened. "What have I done?" I thought.'

But it was not the first time an Aboriginal voice had been raised to use the written word as a means of effecting positive change in the deteriorating situation. David Unaipon (1929), author of *Native Legends*, had given a lecture in Melbourne (July 1914) to the Royal Geographical Society. What he maintained was relevant to Aborigines in general. He claimed that his particular tribe, the Narrinyeri, was not doomed—contrary to popular belief—and that, although it was obvious the tribe was decreasing in numbers, the onus was upon the white authorities to reverse the situation since it was their methods of 'protecting' which were causing the demise.

Unaipon was a man who had a proven inventive genius for mechanics. It had been for reasons of furthering this scientific knowledge which led him to embark upon, as he puts it, 'a walkabout among the white race' (nd, 19). University professors and students received him warmly (though not without interested curiosity) but, Unaipon (nd, 20) says:

> Later, it occurred to me that I might take me a course of lecturing on the Aborigines, and while going round the country awaken interest in the Aboriginal problem by selling some literature on the subject. I wrote up some legends for this purpose.

His first published legend appeared in the journal *The Home* in February 1925, entitled 'The Story of the Mungingee', which tells how the constellation commonly known as the Pleiades came into being. The essence of the story is that the Mungingee, or Pleiades, were once a group of adolescent Aboriginal girls whose courage and determination in overcoming extreme trials, were honoured by 'the Great Spirit. ...They were transferred to the heavens without death or further suffering that they might shine there as a guide and symbol to their race' (1925, 43).

The real strength of the legend, however, lies in the suggestiveness that evolves out of Unaipon's reduction of Aboriginal legend to European short story. Or possibly, as John Beston (1979, 341) observed, 'the Christianizing of the legends enabled Unaipon to gain the interest of his audience without alienating them by presenting values other than their own'. But in his reduction of the intricacies of Aboriginal lore and ritual to prose, Unaipon had not relinquished the intrinsic prescriptive quality of the legend for the sake of illustrating how his people can achieve the sort of salvation or redemption which the modern white critic believes lies behind Christianising the material.

The point is, if, as Beston (1979, 341) himself claims, David Unaipon is capable of asserting in his legends that 'Aboriginal values are as worthy of respect as those of any other society, including a Christian society', then there is an inherent negation of the prejudices and derogatory attitudes held by non-Aborigines toward blacks and anything associated with them. The level upon which Unaipon (1925, 42) wants the audience to absorb 'The Story of the Mungingee', for example, is undoubtedly established in the introduction, where he writes:

> According to legend it was the 'Yartooka' who, in the early days of my race, perceived the necessity for the submission of the body to the mind—a submission that would mean the restraint of physical appetite and the effects of pain and fear. They say that without this there could be no racial advance.

The story surely concerns the astounding endurance of the 'Yartooka' and how this remains an inspiration to Aborigines, but the terms of the writer's introduction impose a further framework (relevant to what is already familiar to the audience) to establish the didactic intention of the author vis-a-vis Western society.

The 'dying-out' syndrome was as prevalent an attitude toward the Aboriginal population in the 1920s as any other decade since white settlement. Unaipon's comments concerning the threat to 'racial advance' would have immediately attracted the interest of most since, as an educated Aborigine, Unaipon was indicating a possible cause for racial regression—a cause that was dissociated from white involvement. The lust for the material and the physical supported the theory that the dying-out was self-inflicted, further (and conveniently) absolving the white community of blame. However, as in his Royal Geographical Society lecture (1929), Unaipon's style exposes inadequacies inherent in the dominant society rather than affirming the misconceptions surrounding his race's survival. By retelling the legend Unaipon was attempting to explain the strong principles that moulded the character of the Aborigines, which, in effect, cast in relief the decaying values and ideals of European civilisation. The previous ten years had witnessed the greatest carnage in the history of humanity. Contained in 'Mungingee' (1925, 43) is a plea by the Yartooka addressed to those of other tribes, after they had successfully completed the trials:

> Greed and pain and fear are caused by thinking too much of self, and so it is necessary to vanquish them. Will you not go and do as we have done?

Now although Unaipon does not presume that the white man will accept that his Aboriginal dependant has something to offer him concerning the timeless problem involving the relationship between intellect and appetite, he does, however, exploit the irony that the Yartooka's triumph over the sort of materialism which produced such barbaric results in the Great War argues for the Aborigine's awareness that solutions to such problems are attainable.

His own interest in a seemingly insoluble problem—namely, the secret surrounding perpetual motion—led him between 1904 and 1909 to develop a mechanism that would improve the performance of sheep shears. According to David Jenkin (1979, 235), Unaipon was to take out a total of nineteen applications for patents from 1909 to 1944, and 'was still wrestling with mechanical problems and theories practically till the day he died' in 1967. But as Unaipon (nd, 20) himself explained in his address to the Annual Meeting of the Aborigines' Friends' Association (AFA):

> While some people regarded my attempt to find out the secret of perpetual motion as a dream, the instrument I often took with me to illustrate my studies, appealed to many of the educated, and this enabled me also to interest them in the welfare of the Aborigines.

Jenkin (1979, 235) corroborates this but seems to relate what a polite Unaipon, could not be expected to say given the circumstances:

> In his later years (Unaipon) was to use his ingenious mechanical devices...for propaganda purposes. People would attend his advertised lectures to see the remarkable machines in action, and in fact they would see them. But they would also be given a lecture on the plight of the Aborigines of Australia, and be told what was needed to be done by the dominant race. Nevertheless the inventions were no mere gimmicks.

There was little Unaipon could do about the novelty aspect that surrounded him as an Aboriginal inventor and his display. He could focus attention upon the device itself emphasising its intricacies and hopefully corroding the condescension that exuded from the audience's self-conscious superiority. This in turn would set the level at which Unaipon wanted his audience to appreciate his information. It had to be remembered that the current government policy of 'smoothing the dying pillow' was a direct contradiction to an appreciation of the real value of Aboriginal knowledge, for a dying race was not expected to possess anything of value to an independent, progressive nation.

It is precisely these misconceptions, however, which induced Unaipon to use the opportunities afforded him as an inventor, speaker and writer to speak out for the Aborigines. He never conceded in his writings that his race was dying out and it can be safely assumed that breaking down this misguided belief was his initial task. For with this stigma jeopardising the present, there could only be stagnation for the Aborigines, and encouragement virtually non-existent. Unaipon (nd, 19) himself contends that when he felt ready to learn more of the world outside the Port McLeay Mission, 'efforts were made to detain me', such as being 'put in the cobbler's shop to learn shoemaking'. As already indicated, the public was not prepared to give the Aboriginal voice a serious hearing. Most unattractive would be one which contradicted conventional views or opinions of whites. Gaining the interest of his audience was thus Unaipon's first objective.

When forced to sacrifice specifics (especially of Aboriginal lore) to generalities to achieve this end, there was the usual disadvantage of the work being open to several levels of interpretation. Yet with Unaipon's ultimate aim being the encouragement of a positive outlook in his audience in relation to the Aboriginal situation, such diverse readings—as either fairy-tale, Christian parable, esoteric or purely Aboriginal folk lore—guaranteed an audience for the legends. Furthermore, Unaipon was unperturbed that the legends would have been assured an audience merely because their author was an educated Aborigine. The beliefs that he expounded were their own reassurance that condescension could not prevent the deeper concerns from eventually surfacing. In his AFA address Unaipon (nd, 20) shows a resolute confidence that should be interpreted as evolving from a faith in such beliefs:

> I think...that by my ideals and dreams, as well as by my writings and lectures, I have both directly and indirectly assisted in bringing about better conditions for the aborigines throughout Australia.

Therefore, in regard to the acceptance of Unaipon's writings as a recognisable branch of his total commitment, it is clear that the type of Christian vision, or sequence, the 1970s critic has imposed upon the writer and his work, is governed not so much by what emerges from within each piece, but by what has been brought to them.

The protest or consciousness-raising element within Aboriginal literature therefore begins, not in the mid-1960s as popularly interpreted, but with the writings of Unaipon forty years previously. Why Unaipon's work has not attracted more attention (eg in comparison with later black writers) can be attributed partly to Australian public attitudes which result in ambivalence toward Aboriginal initiatives. Considering the popular myth surrounding the European invasion of Australia—namely the Great South Continent being classified 'Terra Nullius' (vacant land) with only minor, token resistance to the spread of white civilisation—one can visualise the origins of the disturbing dilemma confronting those blacks who were trying to bring about better conditions.

In 1938, for instance, at the height of the drive for Aboriginal citizenship by the Aborigines' Progressive Association (APA), led by Jack Patten and William Ferguson, among other notable Aboriginal figures, one of the many impediments was the incurable certainty in the public mind that this was a white man's country and therefore Aborigines were ineligible for citizenship. This contemptuous rather than apathetic reception by the white community persists into the 1960s, as can be seen in what Kath Walker (Schwenke 1977) recalls motivated her to write 'Aboriginal Charter of Rights':

> 'Aboriginal Charter of Rights' was written because we were then fighting to wipe out the Queensland Aborigines and Torres Strait Islanders Act. We claimed that under the Charter of Rights all people were born free and equal and we were entitled to the same thing. When we took our case to people like Pat Killoran (Queensland State Government official) their answer was that because the Native Affairs Act had been written long before the United Nations Charter of Rights, it takes precedent over the Charter. Therefore, the Aborigines and Islanders *have* no Charter of Rights.

When Walker returned from Adelaide in 1962 after presenting 'Aboriginal Charter' she found that her residence had been broken into and all her clothing destroyed. This she felt was an attempt to intimidate her because, as she says (Schwenke 1977), 'this was the first time they (the whites) realized I was really writing my own poetry. Up till then they were prepared to think that someone else was writing for me.' She had a poem published in the *Realist Writer*, for example, in 1961 entitled 'Companionship' but, unlike the other poets in the magazine, her name was excluded from the list of contents.

To appreciate the reasons why Walker's work is seen (albeit mistakenly) as the beginning of the Aboriginal literary, protest tradition one must first perceive the unwillingness within the wider white community to accept the validity of the Aboriginal voices that had been raised. Such an obstacle discouraged the spread of Unaipon's influence amongst his people. Indeed, the then Department of the Interior tried to manipulate what influence he did exert to counter the 'Day of Mourning' protest organised by the APA. This protest was to coincide with the one hundred and fiftieth celebrations on Australia Day, 1938. Through persistent and inspired leadership, the APA was able to endure such setbacks and must take much of the credit for not allowing the plight of Aborigines to slip into a dormant issue during and immediately following the Second World War. As Jack Horner (1972, 171) observes, Ferguson made sure that the APA was the first Aboriginal organisation 'to demand the interests of members of Parliament'. The influence of the APA's most loyal members was responsible for the creation of new organistions out of the slump that followed Ferguson's death in 1950.

Doug Nicholls, who had had a long, active involvement in the APA was a driving force behind the founding of FCAATSI in 1958. Kath Walker, who would become the state secretary of the Queensland branch, had met another staunch APA member, Herbert Groves, during a trip to Sydney several years earlier. This encounter served to reinforce the commitment that had led Walker to demonstrate against racial discrimination with a bus-load of protestors in a Queensland coastal country town years before. And it had also moved her to join with Doug Nicholls in gaining improved housing for Aborigines and Islanders in the New South Wales Northern Rivers area back in 1938.

It is not surprising, then, that the grievances detailed in the APA's manifesto of 1938, 'Aborigines Claim Citizen Rights!' should emerge again in Walker's 'Aboriginal Charter of Rights'. Two brief examples will suffice to illustrate how, despite more than a quarter of a century separating the publication of these pleas, no improvements had ensued in the position of Aborigines to warrant a deviation from the original claims. With reference to the White Australia policy, and particularly in relation to its endorsement by the Labor Party and trade unions, Patten and Ferguson state in the manifesto that it 'has helped to create a senseless prejudice against us, making us social outcasts in the land of our ancestor!' (Horner 1972, 198). Walker (1964, 41–42) rephrases it: 'Must we native Old Australians/In our own land rank as aliens?'. Similarly, in the closing demands of the manifesto the designers address the reader, 'After 150 years, we ask you to review the situation and give us a fair deal—a New Deal for Aborigines' (Horner 1972, 198). And Walker's poem (1964, 29) compacts the message: 'Give the deal you still deny us'.

Twenty-five years later, however, there were distinct advantages which would draw closer attention to the same messages; not the least being the hindsight of the seasoned Aboriginal activists which enabled them to utilise the potential influence of new phenomena. The most important of these were the waves of social change filtering from abroad highlighting the ascendant position of blacks; and the newsworthiness of events of this kind, to which the media were quick to respond.

Briefly, the black civil rights movement in the United States had become highly effective and widely publicised under the inspirations of Martin Luther King Jr and Malcolm X. Notable achievements of that movement were the Civil Rights Acts of 1957 and 1960, which made it illegal to discriminate in one form or another against blacks in public places. The racial conflict in Little Rock gained instant worldwide news coverage when the President dispatched troops to Arkansas to enforce the 1954 Supreme Court decision to desegregate schools. Meanwhile in Africa, between 1957 and 1963, more than twenty black African countries achieved their independence from colonial rule (*Europa Year Book* 1987). In the early 1960s, most informed Australians were conscious of the indications, if not the mood, of change in spite of the strong conservative ideology of the postwar Menzies era. This prevailing temper, particularly on an international level, cannot be discounted as having had an influence on race relations in Australia (eg in assisting the eventual establishment of the Australian Institute of Aboriginal Studies in 1964).

Seen in this greater, global context, the period was conducive to the first poetry by a black Australian—conducive because the white Australian conscience could no longer completely ignore the pleas of Aborigines as it had done in the past. Walker's poetry was a means of fulfilling this aim. In this respect it had to be popular, political and rhetorical; and it had to be readable, in that Walker did not cloud her viewpoints in language that was beyond the reach of the layperson. One should, therefore, not place too much value on the mere novelty or curiosity aspect which some critics say was responsible for her becoming Australia's then second, highest-selling poet.

Walker's personal promotion of her poetry was also a promotion of the black Australian cause. Her television and newspaper appearances, and the countless public poetry readings were all a new experience for her audiences, that is, more of an education than a novel attraction. For if her audiences were interested in knowing more about the problems and aspirations of blacks in this country, they could gain first-hand knowledge through Walker's books of poetry.

It is the same didactic role of the black writer, which Davis spoke of in February 1983, and which he feels must be sustained; for at the launching of *Kullark/The Dreamers*, Davis concluded that he is glad that it 'is going to help in some regard in making the Aboriginal voice within the wider Australian society'. Davis is, of course, alluding to the black writer's commitment to reconstructing the image of the Aborigine within the larger context of a total restoration of the Aboriginal community as a force within the dominant society. To achieve this the realm of literature naturally allows the writer a comparable range of approaches. In 'The Dreamers', Davis explores the spiritual/psychological continuum engendered in the Dreaming. The domestic background of the extended Aboriginal family portrayed could pass for any poor, white family. But the play draws its strength from the superimposing of historical and Aboriginal Dreaming realities upon an unalienated audience. Its ultimate success rests with the audience's ability to appreciate the profound consciousness evolving from the Dreaming association, and how, through the influence of its eternal dimension, Aboriginality will be sustained beyond the present.

Empathy with the experience of a socially and economically destitute white family enables the wider, white community to enter partially into the psyche of the poor, urban Aboriginal situation. But this comparison falls far short of what the black dramatist desires of his white audience—empathy with the political realities of being black in a white dominated society.

Gerry Bostock attempts to evoke such empathy through 'Here Comes the Nigger'. But if one were to ask Bostock how well he achieves this he would probably say that the most frequent criticism by whites is that racism tends to be overprojected in his play (1985). The basis of their argument is that the play illustrates how black racism is as much a catalyst for social violence as racism practised by whites. But such criticism merely seeks to conceal the larger question behind racism: what makes racism essentially a potent political force? And it is a question which Bostock confronts in the depiction of how the emergence of a sense of black nationhood is a direct result of having to combat oppression in order to exist. Bostock shows that, for the individual not to recognise the survival struggle inherent in the Aboriginal condition, means the individual has succumbed to the often subtle forms of oppression. Consequently, racism, presumably attributable to social causes in particular, attains that political dimension whereby it is used by the ruling sector to maintain economic and cultural dominance in society. Bostock's play is thus as much a political play as it is social, because it questions the principles by which white society continues its suppression of the Aboriginal populace.

Similarly, a play written by Jack Davis about Aborigines during the Great Depression may be inspired by the author's recognition that a representation of this kind has never been undertaken (Bredow 1985). However, the political realities are difficult to ignore. The portrayal of the struggle to survive shows the fate of a people who have been the subject of deliberate attempts by white authorities to nullify Aboriginal social and cultural forces. It is clearly arguable that playwrights, both white Australian and non-Australian, have set plays in this era to capture the psychological devastation caused by the collapse of social and moral standards during such periods.

For Davis, however, the stimulus to produce yet another 'side' of the untold human story evolves ultimately from his conscious commitment to the regeneration of Aboriginal culture. Such commitment in the black writer stems from an awareness of being one of an invaded people struggling to maintain credibility through their Aboriginality in the face of continued oppression.

But it is also a play that strives to fill in those missing gaps, glossed over, if not ignored, in Australian history books. It has germinated from within a consciousness that is fertilised by the political condition of contemporary Aboriginal society. Likewise, the plays by each of the other black playwrights mentioned here, draw their strength from being plays about Aborigines, written by Aborigines, and, plays which are not necessarily written for an elite audience. Such qualifications preserve the writers' intentions which, conveyed either through social or economic motifs, are founded upon the survival of a threatened Aboriginal culture. Thus, even the play which blends the historical panorama of European/Aboriginal contact with specifically modern situations in the lives of blacks—noticeably in *Kullark* and *The Cake Man* (Merritt 1978)—cannot escape from illustrating how poverty of both spirit and material well-being, perpetuated by adverse treatment by whites, continues to hinder black advancement.

The encumbrances acquired from a history of white oppression has caused, as Kevin Gilbert (1980, 3) says, 'a rape of the soul so profound that the blight continues in the minds of most blacks today' which only a totally new and sustained approach involving re-educating blacks themselves can rectify. Naturally white Australia, with its responsibility for causing 'the blight', has been the target of emergent black literature. But increasingly the literature has turned from criticism of this obvious external force and focused more upon priming the black individual for a regeneration of the self. This process, however, demands substantial self-criticism. Unlike some of the more romantic idealisations of Aboriginal life (which were nonetheless viewed as integral for establishing Aboriginal identity), the positive images of blacks are continually counterbalanced by the more realistic manifestations that depict Aboriginality in all its dimensions. Some of the earliest and more effective forms of this self-criticism can be seen in Gilbert's 'The Cherry Pickers' in which black pretentiousness is soundly attacked by other blacks. It continues through Bostock's 'Here Comes the Nigger', the poetry of Gilbert in *People 'Are' Legends* (1978), and more subtly in Davis's *Kullark/The Dreamers* (1982). The exposing of the dangers of assimilation is among the more prominent reasons for pursuing this theme. But perhaps the most engaging aim is to bring blacks themselves to recognise that unless they actively aspire to self-determination they will remain disadvantaged.

To the Aboriginal writer, as to the blacks they write about, the white man cannot be relied upon to rectify the injustices already evident in the past. The onus is therefore upon Aborigines to take the initiative, as Kevin Gilbert (1973) has noted, 'because a white man'll never do it'. One thus sees that the consciousness-raising which is pivotal to positive change is aimed not only at white society but, of equal significance, at black society as well. Thus in terms of where Aboriginal culture stands today, and its potential future, it is necessary to define the writers' approach not by romantic parameters, nor those of pessimism. It must begin by interpreting the fundamental objective of each as writing for their people—whether this entails describing with imaginative freedom the latent *joie de vivre* of Aboriginality or portraying the inescapable traumas associated with being black. Manifest in the works of the writers are depictions of the various and changing states of Aboriginal consciousness across this human spectrum.

References

Beston, J.
1979 'David Unaipon: The First Aboriginal Writer (1873–1967)', *Southerly*, **39**, 337–42.

Bostock, G.
1980 *Black Man Coming*, privately printed, Melbourne.
1985 'Black Theatre', in J. Davis and B. Hodge (eds), *Aboriginal Writing Today*, Australian Institute of Aboriginal Studies, Canberra.

Bredow, S.
1985 '*No Sugar*, Reflects Sour Struggle', *Weekend Australian*, 23–24 February, 10.

Davis, J.
1970 *The First Born and Other Poems*, Angus and Robertson, Sydney.
1982 *Kullark/The Dreamers*, Currency Press, Sydney.

Europa Year Book
1987 Europa Publications, London.

Gilbert, K.
1970 'The Cherry Pickers', typescript, Australian National Library, MS 2584.
1971 *End of Dreamtime*, Island Press, Sydney.
1973 *Because a White Man'll Never Do It*, Angus and Robertson, Sydney.
1978 *People 'Are' Legends*, University of Queensland Press, St Lucia.
1980 *Living Black*, Allen Lane, Ringwood, Victoria.
1984 Personal correspondence with author, 2 April.

Horner, J.
1972 *Vote Ferguson for Aboriginal Freedom*, Australian and New Zealand Book Company, Sydney.

Jenkin, G.
1979 *Conquest of the Ngarrindjeri*, Rigby, Adelaide.

Merritt, R.
1978 *The Cake Man*, Currency Press, Sydney.

Schwenke, J.
1977 Interview with Kath Walker, Brisbane.

Unaipon, D.
nd *My Life Story*, Aborigines' Friends' Association, Adelaide.
1925 'The Story of the Mungingee', *The Home*, 1 February, 42–43.
1929 *Native Legends*, Hunkin, Ellis and King, Adelaide.

Walker, K.
1961 'Companionship', *Realist Writer*, 7, 6.
1964 *We Are Going*, Jacaranda Press, Brisbane.
1966 *The Dawn is at Hand*, Jacaranda Press, Brisbane.

'The Coming of the Dingoes'— Black/White Interaction in the Literature of the Northern Territory

David Headon

In the 1982 Australian film, *We of the Never-Never*, Angela Punch-Macgregor, as Mrs Aeneas (Jeannie) Gunn, emerges as the archetypal turn-of-the-century pioneering white woman: feminine, but hardy; strict with her helpers, but with a heart of gold; and emotionally strong, if the occasion demands, yet passionate. It is a faithful portrayal of the central character in Mrs Gunn's novel, on which the film is based. For Mrs Gunn, life at Elsey Station, just south of Katherine in the year 1902, is generally an uninterrupted bush idyll. Elsey nights are 'singularly beautiful...shimmering with warm tropical moonlight' (1982, 17). In the exotic 'Never-Never', Mrs Gunn's Aborigines learn to appreciate the white man's energy and tolerance, his sense of brotherhood and the civilising effect of British territorial expansion.

We of the Never-Never fairly represents a substantial section of this country's white pioneering literature, including that issuing from the Northern Territory frontier. Yet, when one compares Jeannie Gunn's North with that of Xavier Herbert, in his classic novel, *Capricornia*, obvious differences emerge. In Chapter One of *Capricornia*, 'The Coming of the Dingoes', the actions of Captain Edward Krater, a trepang fisherman, and his men, far from contributing to the benevolent march of Empire, result in confusion and killing. The indigenous population, the Yurracumbungas, experience the full brunt of Ned's ferocity and violence. The man they label Munichillu, the Man of Fire, is initially welcomed by the Yurracumbungas as a superman come to rule, a teacher of magic arts. They soon learn otherwise. The chapter ends with the white trepanger's slaying of Kurrinua, the Yurracumbunga leader, as the Aborigine performs his own death corroboree. Ned Krater shoots, then spits. We are catapulted into the grim and savage world of Herbert's last Australian frontier.

The accounts of Gunn and Herbert are diametrically opposed. Gunn's fertile haven is Herbert's wasteland—of landscape and of the spirit. When Gunn's husband, the maluka, dies of malarial dysentery at book's end, his belief in God's presence 'Behind all Shadows', even at the last (1982, 238), is unshakable. So, too, is his wife's faith. All mourn, with dignity and decorum, 'the best Boss that ever a man struck' (1982, 238). By contrast, death in

Herbert's chaotic hinterland is suitably macabre. 'Eyes—nothing but eyes—eyes—bulging and horrified!' (1943, 200). This is our last image of Joe Ballest after he's hit by a train. When Jock Driver is buried in a monsoonal downpour, amidst hiss and gurgle of bubbles, the assembled mourners bail against the tide, determined that they should be attending a burial, rather than a drowning.

Whether one considers character portrayal, depiction of the landscape, or even philosophy, there is little common ground between Gunn and Herbert. When one considers, in the novels of both authors, the far more complex and important question of the interaction between Aborigines and Europeans in the north, there is no common ground at all. Gunn's Aborigines are the willing and grateful beneficiaries of white largesse. Herbert's Aborigines in *Capricornia* and in *Poor Fellow My Country* (1975), are appallingly treated by the Europeans. They are at best discriminated against; at worst, hunted, brutalised and slaughtered. A survey of a century of white literature of the north, up to the last decade or two, broadly reinforces the validity of Gunn's depiction of black/white relationships.

This chapter, in support of the honesty of Herbert's provocative metaphor, 'the coming of the dingoes', will dispute the weight of evidence in white literature. I want to concentrate on some of the strategies of dishonesty and disguise perpetrated by these works, in order that, as Bob Hodge (1984, 86) has put it when discussing a Jack Davis play, 'the old lies should not go unchallenged'. When Dee Brown's extraordinarily moving *Bury My Heart at Wounded Knee* (1970) was published over seventeen years ago, it had enormous world-wide exposure. In Australia, we probably felt the book's impact as much as any country outside America. When I was young, 'Cowboys and Indians' was inevitably the game, and no one wanted to be the Indian—the sneak, the savage, the loser. Having a game of 'Settlers and Aborigines', I might add, was not even thought of—such was the extent of American influence on our media in the 1950s.

Bury My Heart at Wounded Knee exploded myths. Indian account after Indian account, courtesy of the records of the treaty councils and other formal meetings between Indian and US government officials last century, testify to a terrible catalogue of white intrigue, coercion, dishonesty and murder. Yellow Wolf, a crack warrior of the Nez Perces, put it as well as anyone cited in the history when he suggested in 1877 that:

> The whites told only one side. Told it to please themselves. Told much that is not true. Only his own best deeds, only the worst deeds of the Indians, has white man told (Brown 1970, 316).

Dee Brown's account of this 'conquest of the American West as the victims experienced it' has clear implications for our own frontier literature. With notable exceptions, including Xavier Herbert, whites in Australia have told only one side. While it is not possible at this stage to piece together a coherent history based on Aboriginal oral, and written, testimony, it is certainly possible to construct an argument which calls to account those white writers, like Jeannie Gunn, who have determined to celebrate the civilising effect of white culture and refinement, while conveniently ignoring its barbarous underside.

I want to dwell on the reality of this underside, comparing and contrasting European and Aboriginal accounts. For the record, this simply would not have been possible as recently as ten years ago because of the paucity of Aboriginal sources available. It can now be done, thanks to the publication, in recent years, of books such as Grant Ngabidj's *My Country of the Pelican Dreaming* (Shaw 1981), Paddy Roe's *Gularabulu* (1983) and *Reading the Country* (Benterrak et al 1984), Jack Sullivan's *Banggaiyerri* (Shaw 1983), John Cribbin's *The Killing Times* (1984), Jampijinpa's account in *Warumungku Watikirli* (Nash 1984), *Fighters and Singers: The Lives of Some Australian Aboriginal Women* (White et al 1985), and *This is What Happened* (1986), the Hercus and Sutton edited series of historical narratives by Aborigines. Add to this the superb collection of oral testimonies put together by Jay and Peter Read (nd) in their unpublished 'A View of the Past: Aboriginal Accounts of Northern Territory History', and the variety of oral material now available in the land claim books, and there emerges an impressive and growing collection of narratives. These are at once history and literature, which collectively act as an appropriate and damning corrective to the scores of white fiction and non-fiction accounts.

Four points need brief mention. First, when discussing Aboriginal literary works relevant to the Northern Territory, it is not a simple task to establish demarcation lines. Aboriginal testimony, alas, does not respect white arbitrary state borders. Material used will spill over into other states, into adjoining areas in South Australia, Western Australia and Queensland. New South Wales material, or that from states further away, will not be used. Second, I interpret the term 'literature' broadly. The American critic, Vernon Louis Parrington, pointed out in his landmark study, *Main Currents in American Thought* (1927, vi–vii), that American literary historians held an 'exaggerated regard for aesthetic values', thus ignoring the literature of 'material struggles' and 'vigorous polemics'. The same is true of Australia, except that here the belletristic preoccupation has lasted longer and still exists. Analysis of Northern Territory literature cannot avoid the inclusion of what Parrington terms 'old-fashioned beef and puddings' material. Thirdly, I intend to progress, in this discussion, from examination of theme, to contextual matters, to a brief look at those factors affecting the availability of Aboriginal material—in particular, the difficulty of getting effective translation onto the written page. Some rather dubious claims have been made about Aboriginal, white and contact literature in Australia in recent years which simply fail to withstand careful and honest scrutiny. Now, as much as ever, we need clarity, commitment and truth.

Mrs Gunn's *We of the Never-Never* celebrates her notion of the humanitarian aspects of Empire expansion, arms outstretched to indigenous peoples as a gesture of goodwill; indeed, in one chapter she sermonises on the need to treat blacks fairly and allow them the right to travel. The book is a product of its time, but even allowing for this, a number of references are disturbing. In Chapter 20, for example, she introduces us to the phrase 'niggers in', which generally means 'cattle-killing'. As a result of herd losses, the maluka and his men head out on what is labelled a 'nigger-hunt'. Mrs Gunn assures us that this will only involve, in her words, 'general discomfiture' for the captured. Now this is curious, because Alfred Searcy, a friend of the Gunns and sub-collector of customs in the Northern Territory from 1882–96, provides a quite different perspective on the Aboriginal hunts of his mate Aeneas, the maluka. In his volume of Top-End experience, *In Australian Tropics* Searcy (1909, 29), states that Gunn obtained the information for a newspaper article on pioneering while out bush endeavouring to 'pot some desperate niggers'. For Mrs Gunn's 'general discomfiture', perhaps we should read 'casual butchery'.

We of the Never-Never typifies the maternalism and paternalism, ignorance and crafty exploitation of euphemism characterising so much of the written history of white settlement in the north, and its accompanying literature. Confusion, misrepresentation and lies abound. Arthur Phillip, when he sailed to the new southern continent with a shipment of white prisoners in 1787, carried with him instructions to 'endeavour by every possible means to open an intercourse with the natives, and to conciliate their affections...' (Powell 1982, 39). Some of his successors took this policy seriously, even in the north—Captain Collett Barker, for example, the last commandant at Fort Wellington before its abandonment in August, 1829 (Powell 1982, 53). But such men were the exceptions. More often, as WEH Stanner remarks, in Australia's early years:

> insensibility towards the Aborigines' human status hardened into contempt, derision and indifference. The romantic idealism, unable to stand the shock of experience drifted through dismay into pessimism about the natives' capacity for civilization (Urry 1985, 51).

The degree to which white community attitudes had hardened in the mid-nineteenth century, can be gauged by the editorial of Sydney's *Empire* newspaper (30 January 1851). Edited by Henry Parkes, the *Empire* was arguably Australia's most liberal newspaper of the period. Acclaiming the sixty-third anniversary of white settlement, Parkes maintained that:

> the sable Australian...never got beyond a kangarooo hunt (note the past tense), or an ascent up a gumtree for an opossum, never contrived a defter thing than his triangular-shaped sheet of bark, or his boomerang of plain-cut miall. And yet with all this mental imbecility, this remarkable inferiority in the human being. ...Australia has risen to a position to command the attention of every civilized nation of the earth.

Throughout Australia, philanthropists anticipated Aboriginal extinction; misanthropists hastened it. David Syme's Melbourne *Age* solemnly declared in 1858 that readers could at best 'smooth the pillow of a dying race' (Inglis 1974, 166).

White expectation of and speculation on extinction of the Aboriginal population only began to subside in the 1920s; in the north the date was later than that. Little wonder, then, that under such conditions the more undesirable elements in the white Territorian community felt emboldened to parade their unashamedly savage ways, usually under the guise of God's assistant—whether white trepanger, pastoralist, explorer or government official. The Territory's Government Resident in the 1860s, Boyle Travers Finniss, an ex-British army officer, sent a punitive expedition out with instructions to 'shoot every bloody native you see' (Powell 1982, 80). The pattern was set.

Jay and Peter Read, in their 'View of the Past' (nd, 25), cite both black and white informants as having reported killings and massacres at Wave Hill, Gan Gan, Tempe Downs, Undooly, Macarthur River, Victoria River Downs, Delamere, Murray Downs, Oenpelli and Killarney. Furthermore, there were three 'official' punitive expeditions: at Barrow Creek in 1874; at Daly River in 1884; and Coniston in 1928. Jasper Gorge in 1895, also seems to have been officially condoned. An analysis of these massacres, and the literature that has resulted, is revealing. Generally, the moving Aboriginal accounts of the killings, some at first-hand, especially those delivered with potent simplicity in Aboriginal English, bear stark contrast to the laboured rhetoric and, at times, sinister prose of the written white responses to the same incidents.

When two men were killed by Kaititja men at the Barrow Creek telegraph station in 1874, the first official punitive expedition, under Samuel Gason, was organised. The Adelaide *Advertiser* trumpeted revenge. 'Retribution', the leader declared, 'to be useful, must be sharp, swift, and severe' (Powell 1982, 131). It was all that, and more, for the party stayed out bush for two months. Decades later, Philippa Bridges related details of her visit in the 1920s to Barrow Creek in *A Walk-About in Australia* (circa 1925, 202). She maintained that the graves of the slain station master and blacksmith:

> lie in a little enclosure near the compound, and though history does not record that their death has been avenged, a creek called Skull Creek, about half a mile away, might tell a different tale.

Coolly, even brutally objective, Bridges's account is typical of the way many Territorians responded to the large-scale murder of Aborigines. The burial method mentioned, of using a creekbed as a dumping ground in order to dispose of evidence, would prove to be a popular tactic in the future.

In the 1880s and 1890s, relations between Europeans and Aborigines rapidly deteriorated as the number of settlers arriving—and thus, confrontations grew. Hostilities worsened. White anger turned more threatening, at times to sadism, individually and collectively, privately and publicly. Groups of white shooters, called in the literature 'quietening' parties, multiplied. Larger and larger areas of the north were 'quietened'. The violence of some settlers at this time—in the privacy of their own stations thousands of kilometres into the Never-Never was quite simply psychopathic. Ivan Egoriffe's actions at Bradshaw's Run, violent and, ultimately, murderous, are made the more terrifying because of the tone of the station journal writer who recorded them (Read 1979, 7):

> 5th October [1899]. Found the runaway Charles Kolomboi, and Ya inbella, chained the former up all night.
> Fri. 6th. Ivan gave Kolomboi the father of a bumping and sent him and the lubra to glory.

How many were like that? Mr Jack Watson, of Lorne Hill, certainly was perhaps worse. Watson, a property owner encountered by Emily Creaghe, Australia's first white female explorer, on her 1883 journey, had lost some cattle, apparently to local Aborigines. His response was to organise a trophy room with, as Creaghe's diary records, '40 pairs of blacks' ears nailed round the wall' (Creaghe nd, 7). As the dispassionate series of entries in Creaghe's diary makes clear, Mr Watson's wall decorations were not considered by his guests as unacceptable. If Ernest Favenc, head of the exploring party, or Mrs Creaghe, or her husband, were even slightly discomfited, she does not record it. A later entry perhaps shows us why. When an Aboriginal girl is caught the next day by the usual method, 'rope round her neck and drag her along from horseback', Mrs Creaghe chronicles her progress during her first day at the station this way (Creaghe nd, 8):

> 31/2/83 The new gin whom they call 'Bella' is chained up to a tree a few yards from the house, and is not to be loosed until they think she is tamed.

'Tamed'. Bella and her people, it appears, are animals. Provided it is accepted that one can treat animals with appalling cruelty, then it follows, according to the logic of some nineteenth century white pioneers, that the indigenous population can be treated that way as well.

The literature in the public area of the period is little better. The official punitive expedition led by Corporal George Montagu, organised in late 1884 to avenge the killing of three white copper miners at Daly River, embarked on its mission with almost total community support in the Territory— hysterical support. No explanation for the original murders is recorded, but whatever the reason, it could scarcely justify the massacre that followed. The Protector of Aborigines in Darwin at the time, Dr RJ Morice, estimated that some one hundred and fifty Mulluk Mulluk and Woolwongas were killed in reprisal (Pye 1976, 7). The local newspaper, the *Northern Territory Times*, captured the mood of its northern readership when it stated that the mistake of the three dead men was to have been 'too kind'. For this they suffered 'at the hands of a race of creatures resembling men in form, but with no more trace of human feeling in their nature than Siberian wolves' (Powell 1982, 132).

The Mulluk Mulluk and Woolwonga peoples were decimated. We have no Aboriginal testimony relevant to the Daly massacre, though we do have, in Hercus and Sutton's *This is What Happened*, some Aboriginal responses to punitive raids of the same time period, near the Koonchera waterhole in South Australia. In 1971, Mick McLean Irinjili reported the tradition of the

Mindiri massacre to Luise Hercus (1986, 189), as he heard it from the last survivor, Charlie Ganabidi. The spare translation is a poignant document. In part it reads:

> They killed all the women, the blind old men and the young initiates, they killed them all at Koonchera.
> 'They never think about running away, shoot'm all down then...'
> They (the police) gave out orders amongst themselves, they told them to stand still, they said, 'let'm all get killed!'—they got killed right as they named the verse, just as they named the verse. 'Let them sing the words of the Mindiri.' 'Let them get killed!' They ordered (in English) 'Let'm get shot!'

The aftermath of the Daly massacre is instructive: for decades to come the Aborigines of the area were labelled merciless savages, as bad as any in the entire Territory.

Unfortunately, the Daly saga does not end with the conclusion of the punitive expedition's activities. Because of the white deaths, a native police corps under mounted constable first class WH Willshire was formed to patrol the Victoria River region. Willshire produced his most elaborate tome to answer his carping critics—the 'rude barbarians' in the south—who considered his methods excessively violent. His book, entitled *The Land of the Dawning: Being Facts Gleaned from Cannibals in the Australian Stone Age* (1896), is full of the protagonist's exploits at the head of 'quietening' parties. On one occasion, in 1894, he and his men came across a large mob of Aborigines in the Victoria River region (1896, 41–42):

> It's no use mincing matters—the Martini-Henry carbines at this critical moment were talking English in the silent majesty of those great eternal rocks. The mountain was swathed in a regal robe of fiery grandeur, and its ominous roar was close upon us. Out from between the rocks came a strapping young girl...the prettiest black girl I ever saw.

This is a representative passage—dispersal and its aftermath, rapturously, poetically rendered. In a work of fiction it would be grim reading. In a work that, as historical sources indicate, was at least based on fact, it is monstrous.

With Willshire in the general area in the 1880s and 1890s, the Aborigines of the Victoria River area would have had a clear idea of the white man's sense of justice and 'civilised' behaviour. But they can hardly have been ready for the consequences of the attack, by some of their number, on the teamsters at Jasper Gorge, near Victoria River Downs, in May 1895. In *Packhorse and Waterhole* (1933, 115–17), Gordon Buchanan describes the actions of the punitive force in familiar language: 'it was fortunate after a long search and by patient tracking to surprise at last a large camp of the enemy and *inflict adequate punishment*'. Reprisals continued. Weeks after the teamsters were attacked, two Bilignara girls working at the Gordon Creek police station persuaded some of their bush people to come in to help build a yard. Mick Inginma, speaking with Peter Read in 1977 (Read and Read, nd, 126–27) takes up the story:

> They come in from the creek. Come out, and puttem chain now longa all
> this mob. ...Well they bin puttem chain now longa neck. Linem up.
> 'Righto. Gottem plenty tea, plenty tucker. Givem a feed.' He bin givem feed
> for last (time).

A little later:

> 'Come on, all you trackers'.
> Makem ready. (Then the policeman said to the prisoners): 'Now, go on!'
> Kickem in the rib, one of them.
> 'All start. Right! Line up!'
> Tu! Tu! Tu! Tu! Tu! Tu! Tu!
> Finish.

After the cunning and expedient fashion of the time, the bodies were heaped
in a creekbed, the burnt remains to be swept away in the next wet season.
Inginma describes the mass cremation this way (Read and Read nd, 126–27):

> All right, chuckem all that there now heap, everything, dog and all. They
> burnem now. They puttem mob of wood, there, type of thing. And chuckem
> kerosene, strike some matches, and burnem. Lot. No anything left, eh? All
> ashes. Burnem finish. Lot.

It is a graphic description; story, and yet with the kind of specific detail
that comprises truth. Further, in this as in all Aboriginal oral testimonies
of the north that I have seen, there is no attempt to criticise or judge. Another
example is the story told to C Boekel and Peter Read by five or six Yaralin
men about the shooting of some old Wadaman, Alura and Djamindjung
people. Replicating the Gordon Creek scenario, some young Aborigines,
station hands, encouraged some of the older people to come into the station,
this time with a lure: 'Gotta lot of tobacco, lot of smoke, matches, tucker,
tea, sugar. You get plenty feed, plenty ration.' The only difference with this
testimony is the more blatant coercion apparently used (Read 1979, 19):

> All this white man, they tell the [black station hands] 'You gotta shoot your
> colour. If you can't shoot 'em, then I've got to shootem you', he said.
> Some men shot in yard, and they gettem big draught horse in yard, puttem
> long chain, and tie up, and drag [the bodies] longa river, puttem in hole,
> strikem matches.

Sophisticated massacre techniques in the north were obviously used widely.
In the van of Christian civilisation, we can conclude, some white community
leaders discussed the more effective ways of dispensing with piles of
murdered men—and women, and children.

The last official punitive expedition, that at Coniston in 1928, being more
recent, is the most extensively documented. The spare details are these: Fred
Brooks, a dingo hunter, was killed by Aborigines at Coniston station. Heading
the punitive party, Mounted Constable William Murray, with two black-
trackers, recruited lessee RB Stafford and three other men. They shot some
Aborigines. After pastoralist 'Nugget' Morton was attacked a short time later,
Murray and Morton shot some more Aborigines (in all, thirty-one, according
to their count).

In the forty odd years since Barrow Creek, community intolerance of the brazen killing of Aborigines had increased, but this did not stop the established white propaganda machine rolling into action once more. Perhaps the most elaborate of a succession of white cover-ups of Coniston comes from Sidney Downer in his *Patrol Indefinite—the Northern Territory Police Force*, published by Rigby over twenty years ago. Chapter 1, 'The First Round-up' begins (1963, 13):

> This is the story of the application of the white man's law, with all its constitutional and statutory complexities, to a land where magic and superstition are still potent forces.

Downer (1963, 119) spends a whole chapter on the Coniston incident. Murray, a Gallipoli veteran we learn, who was wounded four times in action, is a 'resolute man to whom was entrusted the task of bringing in Brooks' murderers'. Downer (1963, 121) portrays Nugget Morton as the perfect complement to Murray: 'No human of lighter metal than this man of iron could have withstood the terrible battering he received'. In the last paragraph of the chapter, Downer (1963, 126) puts his final touches to the whitewash: he informs us of Murray's exoneration and acclaims successful conduct of 'the final war between white men and aborigines in Central Australia'.

Sidney Downer gets one thing right. Murray was cleared. However, Aboriginal testimony, from men and women, places grave doubts on the rest of the story of white heroism. The real story at Coniston, in 1928, what the Walbiri refer to as 'the killing times', does not place the central white figures in the drama in such a favourable light. In translation from the Walbiri, Tim Japangardi Langdon gives his version of the murder of trapper Brooks (Read 1978, 16):

> In the old days there used to be a group of Aboriginals working with Brooks. They were digging a dam and dragging the dirt out with camels. There was an old man who had about three or four wives. Brooks started sleeping with an Aboriginal wife. Then he took one called Martha for three days and threatened the man he would shoot them if they didn't leave him alone. The old men made an arrangement so they could kill Brooks.

The details are clear, even if the translation robs the story of its earthy, human, lived quality. Rosie Nungarrayi's testimony in the Mount Barkly Land Claim document, by contrast, is conspicuous for its honesty, simplicity and clarity. Nugget Morton, we learn, 'was a troublesome bugger' (Wafer and Wafer 1983, 52):

> We were living at Wirliyajarrayi when the troublesome whiteman Nugget Morton Warringari was living at Mud Hut. He shot people in those days. Frightened by him we travelled camouflaged in the scrub bush, drinking from soakages only at night when it was dark and cooler. My relations were murdered by this whiteman, finished by him. We dug for *yarla* [bush yams] and gathered *yakajirri* [currants].

When compared to this testimony, so descriptive and innocent, the atrocities hidden by white rhetorical language tools are focused more sharply. Milly

Nangala supplies additional domestic detail in her testimony (Wafer and Wafer 1983, 55):

> At that time, the people were performing a ceremony for making young men. ...The women were singing: '*Kardarrarra, Kardarrarra*' when the white men came shooting.

Aboriginal men such as Martin Jampijinpa, Johnny Nelson Jupurrulu and Neddy Jakamarra, when discussing Coniston, tend to concentrate on the details of the shootings. 'Round 'em up, just like cattle', was the way Martin Jampijinpa summed up the horrors of Coniston in a 1977 interview, 'and bringem to one mob this way just suddenly. And shot it there' (Cribbin 1984, 161). Neddy Jakamarra injects about as much passion into his statement as the emotions will allow (Cribbin 1984, 163):

> All our mob been shot. My grandmother Maryanne...bin die poor bugger. A lot of people bin shot there. Working man, too. All the working man bin shot too. You know, they bin go to corroboree.

Jimmy Jungarrayi's testimony resembles the white accounts, being less specific, more inclined to overview. But there the similarities cease. While the white literature characteristically condemns black treachery as it eulogises white resolve, Jungarrayi dwells on the extent of the tragedy, no specific blame, with restraint and dignity. He remembers only with immense compassion for the victims (Read and Read nd, 112a):

> And they bin turnem round, and shootem all. All people all, like bullock. Old people bin here, this country. Old people, like bullock. Big mob, woman, kid, man. Too much woman. Too much...too much man. Too much blackfeller. All Walpiri you know, all Walpiri. Poor bugger.

It comes as no surprise to learn in the 'Ti Tree Land Claim' book, in a 1930s statement of Ernestine Hill, of *The Territory* (1951) fame, that in the immediate post-Coniston period, 'to whisper the name Murri to the Lower Territory today is enough to turn the stockboys pale with fright and send the myalls in a wild scatter for the bushland...Murray's name [is] a catchword with which the lubras frighten their piccaninnies today' (Green et al 1984, 25).

When one works through the relatively small corpus of Aboriginal contact literature of the Northern Territory and its surrounds, certain common features emerge. One is the murder, by white revenge parties, of the wholly innocent. A second common feature is an emphasis on the impact, or more accurately, the mythology of European guns. Historian Alan Powell (1982) establishes the white settler's reliance, in his 'quietening' of the hinterland, on the fast-reloading, highly accurate Terry and Snider rifle and the six-shot revolver. The old flintlock muskets were clumsy weapons, a more realistic match for spears. Many cattlemen at the turn of the century made liberal use of the new technology. Daly Bulgara, a Ngarinman living at Yarralin, graphically records a time when some bush Aborigines made first contact with Europeans (Read and Read nd, 34):

Them bloody—whatsa—Europeans come on after that. Banging, banging time now. They [the Aborigines] didn't know that, they reckon some lightning somewhere. ...Another bloke drop. Yeah, bang! Another bloke drop. Bang! 'nother bloke. They bin looking at, you know, they bin looking eye. Something wrong? Got a blood come through nose. 'Oh, might be lightning'. Bang! See? They didn't catch on for a while.

On the third common feature, the abuse of Aboriginal women by white men, both conservative white writer and more radical black storyteller agree. Fred Brooks, the 'troublesome bugger' at Coniston, is merely the most publicised of a prolific white Territory breed who responded to Aboriginal women with lust, harassment and violence. In the first decades of white settlement it was a chronic problem. A Wangaaybuwan descendant recently put it succinctly, and with typical restraint, when he said, 'Our grandmothers were taken advantage of' (Donaldson 1979, 64). In the Territory, more ominously, Jessie Litchfield, a powerful conservative influence on Top End social and political life earlier this century as a journalist and sometime editor of the *Northern Territory Times*, has one of the characters in her novel *Far-North Memories* say (1936, 56):

> Fully nine out of every ten murders in the North have been due, directly or in part, to the unauthorized interference with gins. Not all the true facts ever get into print, of course, but those who have been privileged to peep behind the scenes know more than the general public can ever know or will ever want to know.

This is a remarkable admission from a writer generally given to reactionary public and private statements, and a rare example of white truth-telling in the north. But even her truth is shrouded in the language of the court, the whole ugly story only inferred.

The final element common to Aboriginal contact literature—and, again in this case, white literature—is an emphasis on the importance of the black-tracker's part in the deaths of so many bush Aborigines. As we might expect, arrogant whites such as Alfred Searcy and Willshire point with delight to the strong supportive role played by trackers in quelling the black Territory population. Aboriginal testimony confirms that such men rarely had to be coerced into playing an active role in punitive expeditions. Both Hercus and Sutton, and Richard Broome in his *Aboriginal Australians* (1982), cite specific evidence of this. The most disturbing example of the mentality of some black-trackers, however, occurs in the Reads' 'View of the Past'. Fred Booth Minmienadgie, a Kotanji living at Brunette Downs, in 1977 related the details of a punitive expedition in which he took an active part, south of Tennant Creek, in about 1917. Peter Read suggests in his prologue that it is 'uncertain' whether Minmienadgie was coerced into participating. The man's own testimony suggests he needed little prompting. He takes up the story, with apparent enthusiasm, even bravado (Read and Read nd, 32):

> The wild blackfeller. Oh, shot him, half a hundred. Just about night-time, one bastard run away. I shot him on the leg, fall arse over head.
> 'Where's some blackfeller?' old sergeant said.

'I shot one feller over here, crawl about on his knee. I must have broken his knee.'
'Oh, good. Where's 'nother fellers?'
'I shot him in the bloody head. Oh, he's in the creek, I think'.

Tragically, both Minmienadgie's language and actions imitate his white employers. It is a passage which strongly recalls a scene in the film *Chant of Jimmie Blacksmith*, when Jimmie takes up the policeman's cudgel in one of his numerous pathetic attempts to impress his white role models.

I have drawn attention to the quality and inherent truth of much of the Aboriginal contact literature available. The material in Aboriginal English, especially, has a vigor heightened by compassion, restraint and a certain lived quality which pervades the often sombre yet powerful testimonies. It is one aspect of a burgeoning literature which, along with mythic and song material, makes a mockery of Frederick Macartney's embarrassing, racist claims in his well-known article, 'Literature and the Aborigines' (1957, 59). Macartney exerted considerable influence on the directions of criticism in this country in the 1940s and early 1950s. His articles have not aged well. The piece on Aborigines must rate as the low point in the history of Australian literary criticism, a scurrilous reminder of a forbidding time in this country's intellectual history. It is a poorly researched effort, too. The author does make one accurate observation (though he stumbles onto it for the wrong reasons), when he questions the quality of the early publications by whites of Aboriginal legends—books such as Catherine Langloh Parker's *Australian Legendary Tales* (1896). Bob Hodge (1984, 87), more recently, takes this point up with far greater trenchancy. He questions:

> the coffee-table book of myths or legends, where the rich indeterminancy of the Aboriginal form has been simplified down to a bare, child-like prose, in grammatically perfect but stunned language.

The argument is pertinent to the whole issue of Aboriginal texts today, both in translation and in Aboriginal English. It may not be possible for the translator or transcriber to convey the full impact of the original, but this should not discourage a meticulous study of textual and contextual tools available. Too often in Australian texts, as Colin Johnson (1985, 22) has pointed out, 'the form of the tale or story has been completely neglected. In the process of editing, the oral form has been divorced from the content.' Rarely in the contact literature has there been an attempt to convey nuances of voice, narrative gestures, perhaps even mime, when getting the spoken word on to the page.

Stephen Muecke's efforts here, in Paddy Roe's *Gularabulu* (1983) and *Reading the Country* (Benterrak et al 1984), are excellent examples of what can be done if the task is approached with integrity and persistence. Both texts, especially *Gularabulu*, come near to what American poet and translator David Antin (Rothenberg 1972, xx) has termed 'reality at white heat'. Roe's yarning style pulsates with life because Muecke strives, as editor, to be as silent as the form allows. Many editor/translators over the years have been less than successful in their efforts to do the same. The literature is full of clanger translations—the last line of Billy Thomas-Wombi's 'Air Raid on Broome' (Brandenstein and Thomas 1974, 29) for example, where the Aboriginal speaker, with British lilt, reacts to 'Those chaps with the protruding eyes'; the chant rhythm, in Harney and Elkin's (1949, 37) *Songs of the Songmen*, beginning in the style of the English lyric, 'Oh, list to this story we sing of day'; Luise Hercus's (1977, 62) translation of Rib-Bone Billy's experience, when the protagonist, having just witnessed the slaying of his wife by a white, exclaims, 'Alas, they killed her just like that, I'm bereaved'; or in *Warumungku Watikirli*, when Murtata (Nash et al 1984, 29), confronted by the notorious Constable Murray, can only murmur, in translation, 'Truly he's going to shoot me'. I could continue indefinitely with examples which are equally painful. Either the white translator inadvertently addresses a white audience, or the Aboriginal storyteller does, as in Jack Mirritji's *My People's Life* (1976).

Quite simply, the material available in translation comes a long second to the texts in Aboriginal English. Stephen Muecke (Roe 1983, iv) correctly draws attention to Aboriginal English as 'a vital communicative link between Aboriginal speakers of different language backgrounds'. He goes on: 'It is...in this language that aspects of a new aboriginality could be said to be emerging'. Certainly the finest Aboriginal contact material from the Territory that we have at present is in this form—from early examples in Bill Harney's *Tales of the Aborigines* (nd), to one-off passages such as Pincher Numiari's gritty speech quoted in Gilbert's *Because a White Man'll Never Do It* (1973), to the vitality of Paddy Roe's life and living (1983; Benterrak et al 1984). Perhaps the best illustration of the value of Aboriginal English is Barnabas Roberts's story, given to Margaret Sharpe in 1967 and published in Hercus and Sutton's *This is What Happened*. Roberts's Roper Creole/English testimony of violent contact between Aborigines and whites, and Sharpe's Alawa translation of a related incident are placed back-to-back. Even the translator admits that the Aboriginal English is 'fuller than the Alawa version (in translation) in some respects' (Hercus and Sutton 1986, 63). It certainly is.

I do not think Aboriginal literature is well-served by the rash of dubious generalisations which have become something of a fashion of late—especially in the collection *Aboriginal Writing Today* (Davis and Hodge 1985). It is a fine work, and a really significant addition to the field, but a few of the claims contained between its covers are, at least, debatable. Colin Johnson, for example, in an otherwise perceptive article, suggests that 'perhaps the most that can be said for modern Australian literature, or rather current literature, is its utter complacency and the fact that it is becoming more and more irrelevant to the society with which it seeks to deal' (1985, 28). This is a contentious claim, confronted by the recent work of writers such as White, Keneally, Astley, Jolley, Carey, Malouf, Mathers, Farmer, Zwicky, Dawe, Murray, Herbert, Gray, Hibberd, Williamson, Hewett, d'Alpuget, Garner and many others.

Bruce McGuinness and Denis Walker (1985, 44) declare that unless Aboriginal people control the funding, content, publishing and ultimate presentation of an article, then it is not Aboriginal. Given some of the abominable editing jobs by whites in the past, they have a point. But carried to an extreme, the argument is impractical and, ultimately, negative. It disenfranchises virtually everything presently available.

Davis and Hodge (1985, 6), in their introduction, maintain that it would be wrong to see Aboriginal literature as a part of white Australian literature. I hope my arguments have reinforced that claim. Colin Johnson (1985, 27–28) takes the argument a little further, however, when he says, that Aboriginal literature should not be compared to the dominant English literature but to Fourth World literatures. I believe he's right—in part. A Fourth World comparison is a good idea, but it should not be at the expense of an English/Australian literature context. In the cross section of works I've looked at—the Paddy Roe material, the Read-edited testimonies, the superb content from Aboriginal women in *Fighters and Singers*—all rank highly as important contributions to Australian literature.

Amy Laurie (White et al 1985, 89) in *Fighters and Singers*, finishes her testimony with impressive clarity—proud, yet concerned. It is a novel of epic proportions in just eight lines:

> I reckon they had a good mind these people round here, my countrymen; not like the cheeky mob—cheeky yet. I hear young people like my grandchildren say, 'We bin really silly bugger.' 'What for?' I ask them. 'Well, they never did anything to white man, who kicked him, knocked him out— everything. No nothing—no fight.' Old man black-fellers say, 'You know why we bin let'em shoot we. Why? We frightened? No, we never gotim rifle.' And we didn't care, they reckon... 'We can die in our own country.'

Literature of this kind can withstand any comparison.

References

Benterrak, K., Muecke, S. and Roe, P.
1984 *Reading the Country: Introduction to Nomadology*, Fremantle Arts Centre Press, Fremantle.

Brandenstein, C.G. and Thomas, A.P.
1974 *Taruru: Aboriginal Song Poetry from the Pilbara*, Rigby, Adelaide.

Bridges, P.
c1925 *A Walk-About in Australia*, Hodder and Stoughton, London.

Broome, R.
1982 *Aboriginal Australians: Black Response to White Dominance 1788–1980*, George Allen and Unwin, Sydney.

Brown, D.
1970 *Bury My Heart at Wounded Knee*, Holt, Rinehart and Winston, New York.

Buchanan, G.
1933 *Packhorse and Waterhole*, Angus and Robertson, Sydney.

Creaghe, E.
nd 'Transcript of Diary of Mrs Emily Creaghe', Mitchell Library, MS 2982, Item 1.

Cribbin, J.
1984 *The Killing Times*, Fontana/Collins, Sydney.

Davis, J. and Hodge, B. (eds)
1985 *Aboriginal Writing Today*, Australian Institute of Aboriginal Studies, Canberra.

Donaldson, T.
1979 'Translating Oral Literature: Aboriginal Song Texts', *Aboriginal History*, **III (i)**, 63–67.

Downer, S.
1963 *Patrol Indefinite: The Northern Territory Police Force*, Rigby, Adelaide.

Gilbert, K.
1973 *Because a White Man'll Never Do It*, Angus and Robertson, Sydney.

Green, J., Hagen, R., Spierings, J. and Young, E.
1984 'Ti Tree Land Claim', September.

Gunn, A.
1982 *We of the Never-Never* (London, 1908), Hutchinson, Sydney.

Harney, W.E. (Bill)
nd *Tales from the Aborigines*, Roy Publishers, New York.

Harney, W.E. and Elkin, A.P.
1949 *Songs of the Songmen: Aboriginal Myths Retold*, F.W. Cheshire, Melbourne.

Herbert, X.
1943 *Capricornia* (Sydney, 1938), Appleton-Century, New York.
1975 *Poor Fellow My Country*, Collins, Sydney.

Hercus, L.
1977 'Tales of Nadu-Dagali (Rib-Bone Billy)', *Aboriginal History*, **I (i)**, 53–76.

Hercus, L. and Sutton, P.
1986 *This is What Happened: Historical Narratives by Aborigines*, Australian Institute of Aboriginal Studies, Canberra.

Hodge, R.
1984 'A Case for Aboriginal Literature', *Meridian*, **III (i)**, 86–90.

Inglis, K.
1974 *The Australian Colonist: An Exploration of Social History 1788–1870*, Melbourne University Press, Carlton.

Johnson, C.
1985 'White Forms, Aboriginal Content', in J. Davis and B. Hodge (eds), *Aboriginal Writing Today*, Australian Institute of Aboriginal Studies, Canberra.

Litchfield, J.
1936 *Far-North Memories*, Angus and Robertson, Sydney.

Macartney, F.T.
1957 *Australian Literary Essays*, Angus and Robertson, Sydney.

McGuinness, B. and Walker, D.
1985 'The Politics of Aboriginal Literature', in J. Davis and B. Hodge (eds), *Aboriginal Writing Today*, Australian Institute of Aboriginal Studies, Canberra.

Mirritji, J.
1976 *My People's Life*, Milingimbi Literature Centre, Milingimbi.

Nash, D., Spencer, L., Poulson, N. and Laughren, M.
1984 *Warumungku Watikirli*, Walpiri Literature Production Centre, Yuendumu.

Parker, C.L.
1896 *Australian Legendary Tales*, publisher unknown.

Parrington, V.
1927 *Main Currents in American Thought*, Harcourt, New York.

Powell, A.
1982 *Far Country: A Short History of the Northern Territory*, Melbourne University Press, Carlton.

Pye, J.
1976 *The Daly River Story*, Colemans Printing, Darwin.

Read, P.
1978 *A Social History of the Northern Territory*, No 7, Department of Education, Darwin.
1979 *A Social History of the Northern Territory*, No 9, Department of Education, Darwin.

Read, J. and Read, P.
nd 'A View of the Past: Aboriginal Accounts of Northern Territory History', typescript, Australian Institute of Aboriginal Studies Library.

Roe, P.
1983 *Gularabulu: Stories from the West Kimberley*, Fremantle Arts Centre Press, Fremantle.

Rothenberg, J.
1972 *Shaking the Pumpkin: Traditional Poetry of the Indian North Americas*, Doubleday, New York.

Searcy, A.
1909 *In Australian Tropics*, Angus and Robertson, London.

Shaw, B.
1981 *My Country of the Pelican Dreaming: The Life of an Australian Aborigine of the Gadjerong, Grant Ngabidj, 1904–1977*, Australian Institute of Aboriginal Studies, Canberra.
1983 *Banggaiyerri: The Story of Jack Sullivan*, Australian Institute of Aboriginal Studies, Canberra.

Urry, J.
1985 'Savage Sportsmen', in I. Donaldson and T. Donaldson (eds), *Seeing the First Australians*, George Allen and Unwin, Sydney, 51.

Wafer, J. and Wafer, P.
1983 'The Mount Barkly Land Claim', April.

Willshire, W.
1896 *The Land of the Dawning: Being Facts Gleaned from Cannibals in the Australian Stone Age*, Thomas and Co., Adelaide.

White, I., Barwick, D. and Meehan, B.
1985 *Fighters and Singers: The Lives of Some Australian Aboriginal Women*, George Allen and Unwin, Sydney.

Body, Inscription, Epistemology: Knowing Aboriginal Texts

Stephen Muecke

The old men sat assembled in a circle. They beckoned me in, told me to sit down in their midst. They begin to chant.

They sang of the wanderings of the worrupuntja boys who came to Emiana and thence flew to Tukulja. I listened in silence. The old men continued singing. They sang of the boys, how they were plagued by flies, how they wandered amongst white-blossoming ti-tree bushes, over flowering herbs and flourishing grasses, and how they frolicked on the wide plain bordering the Emiana Creek. The boys desired to perform a ceremony. They wished to decorate themselves. They tore off their finger-nails from their thumbs and first fingers; they used the spurting blood to glue on the ceremonial down.

The old men seized my hand. They all struck up the chant-verse:

> With fierce eyes, with glowing eyes,
> they seize the thumb;
> With fierce eyes, with glowing eyes,
> they rip off the nail.

An old man produced a sharp kangaroo bone (ntjala). He stabbed my thumb with it, pushed the bone deeply underneath the nail. He drew the point out; the rest kept up the chant. He thrust it under the nail in a different place. He gradually loosened the thumb-nail. It was slippery with blood. I almost shrieked with pain; the torment was unbearable. I have not forgotten it: the pain was not slight; it was exceedingly great. When the nail had been loosened, he took a sharp opossum tooth, forced it into the living flesh through the base of the thumb-nail, and tore the nail off from behind. Blood spurted over his hand. The men chanted:

> They rip off the nail, they tear
> off the nail;
> Blood flows like a river, rushes
> along like a river.

Then they seized my left hand and removed the thumb-nail in like manner (Strehlow 1947, 112).

This was a northern Aranda man, Makarinja, relating to TGH Strehlow the harsh conditions under which he was allowed to come into possession of his personal *tjurunga*, an event which comes years after his final initiation. Even in the 1930s this ordeal came to be considered too difficult for the young men (Strehlow 1947, 114):

> Nowadays we make a great concession to the young men in our group. We no longer tear off their fingernails. The price is too high; we give the

tjurunga to them at a much lower cost. Besides, the young of the present generation are no longer hardy enough to endure such pain.

What interests me about this text, and what I shall be elaborating upon, is the peculiar configuration of words, bodies and acts of inscription—on bodies—which mark instances of cultural reproduction. These are the conditions under which traditions are reproduced. These conditions take the form of mechanisms by which bodies and words are co-articulated.

In the above text, the old men sing of the travels of the ancestor figures and about how they had a ceremony involving finger-nail removal. As soon as they get to that part of the traditional song-text, they perform the operation on the initiate, while chanting. The traditional actions are thus inscribed on the body of the initiate. He becomes an ancestor figure, and in that transformation can now become the custodian of the *tjurunga*, the sacred objects with their associated texts.

This could be considered as the basic mechanism for the reproduction of Aboriginal texts. I could cite more domestic examples, like the baking of bread being carried out in conjunction with the telling of a traditional story about bread-baking (Harney 1962, 101). As in the above example, the narrative is articulated with a specific desire on the part of the listener(s); the acquisition of the sacred material.

Now, I want to contrast this traditional mechanism with contemporary literary production. Aboriginal writers today would seem to be subject only to Western conditions for literary production and consumption. In the 'transformation' from spoken word and song to written genres; from body to book; from Aboriginal to European ceremony; there are many things that change the whole sense of the events involved. It would be thus extremely difficult to establish any sort of continuity between traditional Aboriginal 'literature' and work by contemporary Aboriginal writers. Yet in many ways critics are trying to establish just these continuities, for political reasons and to renovate written genres.

A paper by Colin Johnson (1985, 21–33), 'White forms, Aboriginal Content', delivered at the first National Aboriginal Writers' Conference in Perth, gives an introduction to the problems associated with traditional Aboriginal literature, in the 'passage' from the spoken to the written forms, though no individual can have in fact passed that way. He anticipates, I think, what will become a movement to reincorporate traditional poetic technique in contemporary writing in English. In fact, both he and Archie Weller have produced 'song-cycles' which draw on that traditional verbal art-form.

I have already stopped using the phrase 'traditional Aboriginal literature', in favour of 'traditional Aboriginal verbal art'. I see there being two dangers in the use of the term 'literature' for traditional performances. One is that these may be seen as preliterate, as in some way preceding literary productions, as if these lie at the end of a progression. They could then be seen as unelaborated or unsophisticated, in a comparison which always treats writing as more powerful a medium than speech.

The other danger is a reversal of that progression in which traditional productions might be read retrospectively as 'poetic', in light of what we have already come to understand about literature through written mediums. We need to have ways of understanding verbal performances independently of literary assumptions which inform written genres like the novel, poem and short story—ways which take into account the specifics of verbal performance.

A synthesis of those two problems arises most obviously when traditional Aboriginal performances are marketed for local or overseas production. (I am thinking of performances with music, dance and singing, popularly known as the corroboree.) Often, in these situations the tag 'traditional' comes to mean 'timeless'. In the context of the general promotion of Australian culture, the Aboriginal performances are wheeled on as that-heritage-lost-in-the-depths-of-time-for-which-we-as-a-nation-can-be-proud. This general idea tends to ignore the fact that traditions are still in operation as regional cultures, and that they need support to operate as contemporary lifestyles.

Given that, there remain problems of epistemology, access; problems of how one can get to know what 'traditional Aboriginal verbal art' might be, and this includes how much a white Australian like myself might be allowed to know about this area, why I should act as a mediator of this knowledge, creating it whilst inscribing it, setting up the conditions for reading texts and performances.

Margaret Clunies Ross (1983, 20) treats in some detail the problems of notating traditional performances, whether by means of audio or video-tape, film or writing. She recognises that knowing about or understanding these performances depends precisely on the achievement of an adequate form of inscription:

> Until an elegant means of notating the various elements of Aboriginal performance and presenting them together in written form is developed, our ability to understand and then to analyse the complexities of such performances will be slight.

But through the work of Derrida we know that the written form ('notation') cannot assume ascendancy over spoken 'notations'. Knowledge or truth is not just available through the Western form of inscription, alphabetical writing with diacritical variations. In fact, she suggests earlier in her paper (1983, 17) that Aboriginal people have been in some state of pristine innocence untouched by 'writing'. However, I do not want to turn this around and argue that only the Aboriginal form of inscription leads to 'true' knowledge of the events. That would mean that we would all have to have our thumb-nails removed—this condition for knowing is obviously not part of the academic economy of knowledges within which we work.

What I am interested in, therefore, is the relation between epistemology and conditions of production. Instead of conditions of production, I could say writing and performance, but I want a neutral term, because I consider writing to be a kind of performance too; or performance a kind of writing in the Derridean sense of 'inscription', making traces.

However, in spite of my collapsing of this distinction, I want to go back to contrast the tradition of the realist scientific text of ethnography with a (post)modernist performance style of writing with which I have been associated in my work.

When I work with Paddy Roe of Broome; in northwest Australia, writing down his stories in Broome English (one of his many languages), I see my role as being that of the informed scribe, writing his books (from tape recordings) in such a way that they will be effective in relation to a broad readership—both Aboriginal and non-Aboriginal. I do not see it as part of my brief to back up this work with any sort of ethnographic description of the region, language or traditional society as a whole. I do not want to save all this material for posterity—as valuable and as interesting as it may be— because I have a theoretical problem that I cannot yet see my way around.

This problem is that I see my work as being concerned with the production (and distribution) of texts, not just 'material' or pretextual 'contents'. My work is therefore on the medium of communication, which in the case of Paddy Roe is a kind of literary Aboriginal English. The layout of words on the page is intended to draw attention to the textual nature of cultural production. The text is not supposed to be a window onto the world of Paddy Roe. But if I were working on the ethnographic material, then my work would become more obviously empirical. I would be working on facts and figures, structures and terminologies. The fact that I might produce an ethnographic text out of this would not be seen as relevant to that sort of work. The ethnographic text, however well written, is supposed to function as a reflection of the real—a language used transparently to tell us about the real.

What worries me about the ethnographic text is that it is an artifact produced totally within the economies of European institutions. It is a non-Aboriginal communicative device, and is destined to be read largely by non-Aboriginal people. It paradoxically produces lots of information about traditional societies, but as a text, a language event, it has nothing in common with the Aboriginal modes of verbal performance. Nor is there yet a way of seeing 'performance' in its textuality or its dissemination. This is partly because the scientific pretentions of ethnography reserve for it a purely instrumental function of language.

On the other hand, if one does what I did and produces a written text which is more like performed speech—narratives as they are told—then one runs the risk of being told that the texts represent only a trivial or superficial account of all that store of traditional knowledge which historically precedes such production.

One way to wriggle out of this dilemma is to say that neither sort of book will be adequate to the real. That as long as one emphasises performance, one will miss out on factual detail and interpretation, and as long as one does ethnography, one will miss out on the linguistic aspects of performance style. So I think that one has to look closely at what is being produced and conclude that books are essentially artifacts of their Western contexts, and function almost exclusively in those contexts, particularly in education. Traditional Aboriginal verbal performances may also have a lot to do with education, in the broad sense of creating adults who are responsible for keeping the society functioning. But the way in which these oral texts are produced has nothing to do with the way in which books are produced, which is according to the politics of the inscription of traditional modes of Aboriginal performance.

For example, one can illustrate the difference between the ethnographic text, and the performance narrative. The following story comes from Ronald and Catherine Berndt's *Sexual Behaviour in Western Arnhem Land* (1951, 187–88):

> 'Dʒalbima, a *'nji:ndʒariwu:rlga* 'Waːlaŋ, met me out side the "dormitory" (the single men's hut) under the tree, near the church. I call her *'laːla* (sister). Her husband then was 'Naŋunjari, a *'jariwurik* 'Neiŋgu, whom I call *'boːnji* (father).
>
> She spoke to me saying, "What about you find a boy for me? I want one to copulate with me, I feel the *'mainja* (desire)."
>
> "What will you give me, if I get one for you?" I asked.
>
> "I'll give you a plug of tobacco," she replied.
>
> "Alright," I said, and went to look for a boy. I went all over the camp looking for one, but couldn't find any. They were all working in the garden and around the house.
>
> At last I found 'Namanŋu, a *'jariwurik* 'Mauŋ, whom I call *'maːmam*, mending his trousers.
>
> "Come here, I want you," I said.
>
> He came over to me, "Yes?"
>
> "Now if I ask you something, you say 'Yes' or 'No'," I told him.
>
> "Alright."
>
> "You are my friend," I continued.
>
> "Say on," he said.
>
> "There's a girl here who asked me if I could find a boy for her. Would you mind going or not?" I asked.
>
> He replied, "Thank you very much," and took out a stick of tobacco and gave it to me; so that I had a stick from both the girl and my friend.
>
> "Call her name," he said.
>
> "'Dʒalbima."
>
> "Good," he replied.
>
> "I'll wait for you here," I said. And 'Namanŋu went over to the bushes behind the church, in the same direction as the girl had gone. As I saw him disappearing into the tall grass, I said to myself, "I'm going to spy on him." So I walked quietly over towards where they were, and sneaked in and out through the bushes until I came on them from the back way.

This text is a translation from Gunwinggu, the traditional language of the area. It presents itself in the guise of content—the sort of thing people did at the time—as well as reproducing a certain conversational or interactional style. Stories like this could conceivably be used to construct a literary text, but the Berndts used them in this instance as data. The narrator was a man called Small Ngolaman, and he is called the 'informant', the sense being that his language is being used merely to convey information.

The next passage, from one of Paddy Roe's texts, situates Paddy Roe (1983, 3–4) quite differently as a speaker; he is seen as being the creative source of words. Whether the texts are subsequently read as literature or history, Paddy Roe's voice tends to remain a point of 'authenticity', because this is the other major way in which his voice can be placed according to the mechanisms of Western literary hermeneutics:

> MIRDINAN
> Yeah—
> well these people bin camping in Fisherman Bend
> him and his missus you know–
> Fisherman Bend in Broome, karnun–
>
> we call-im karnun–
>
> soo, the man used to go fishing all time–
> get food for them, you know, food, lookin' for tucker - an' his, his missus
> know some Malay bloke was in the creek, Broome Creek–
> boat used to lay up there–
>
> so this, his missus used to go there with this Malay bloke–
> one Malay bloke, oh he's bin doin' this for–
> over month–
>
> so this old fella–
> come back with fish one day he can't find his missus–
> he waited there till late–
> so he said "What happened to my missus?–
> must be gone fishing ah that's all right" he said–
> so he waited and he come back he got nothing–
> "Where you bin" he said, bloke said to him–
> "Ah I jus' bin walkin' round"–
> "Aah"–
> soo all right next morning he start off again–
> "Mus' be something wrong" this old fella said–
> oh he wasn't old but he was young–
> said "'e must be something wrong"–
> so he went fishing–
> he come back from fishing–
> got all the fish come back–
> so he come back on the other road–
> near the creek, Broome Creek, you know–
> come back round that way–
> when he come back "Hello" he seen this man and woman in the
> mangroves, sitting down–
> oh he come right alongside–
> he seen everything what they doin' (Laughs) you know they sitting down.

This 'authenticity effect' has the danger as well as the possible benefit of creating Paddy Roe as the author of the stories. Authorship is a predominantly Western category which orients criticism of literature toward the subjectivity of the individual creator. But it is possible, and it may empirically be the case, in Aboriginal Australia, that custodianship displaces ownership of songs and stories toward a collective ownership—the idea being that individuals are temporarily in charge of various cultural things by virtue of being in a certain position in the society. They are then, not so much the creators of traditions, but they are repeaters. They may be re-enacting or retracing the steps of ancestors, which includes singing their songs and telling their stories.

This may be more the case with secret and sacred ceremonial texts than with more public varieties. Some song men and women will attribute a song to their 'muse', a familiar spirit, who visits them in their dreams and gives them a song, or a sequence or cycle of songs. The song may then be associated with the name of the man or woman who first sang it. This is the most commonly cited example of artistic specialisation in a set of cultures which are generally held not to have occupational specialists in the arts. Each adult person is likely to hold custodianship responsibilities of part of the general tribal repertoire of cultural tradition. These parts are then put together on the more important occasions for the performance of the traditions.

In the absence of specialised artists in the traditional culture, it is clearly difficult to effect a separation between high and popular culture, or between religion and art. The major division in terms of types of texts is that between the sacred, on the one hand, and public, on the other. Education, or learning how to produce the canonical texts, involves a steady initiation, for the individual, toward the most exclusive texts and rituals. Exclusion is generally organised on the basis of sex and age. If one wished to establish a corollary with, say, English departments in universities, this would be like only being able to look at Chaucer and Shakespeare after getting one's PhD. But the Western method for establishing the exclusiveness of the text is to surround it with an infinite proliferation of commentary.

Using a set of techniques dedicated to the development of the moral self, we use the canonical text as a pretext for talking about our own interests in maintaining a secular bourgeois morality. The Aboriginal technique is rather one of repetition and performance of the canonical text under strictly controlled conditions. The Aboriginal novice is not encouraged, after hearing the sacred text, to explain what he or she might feel about it as in the English department seminar. Instead they are often physically disciplined into remembering it; practices like holding the novice's mouth open and reciting words into it.

Given these vastly different learning conditions, what might it mean to read traditional Aboriginal texts? What is to be done with them if they are appropriated as literature? Should they be kept (by their custodians) for performance alone, in appropriate settings, or should they be disseminated and readapted for contemporary purposes?

If an important part of traditional performance is the creation of memory, via a memorable text, then this might also have important historical and political effects. There are various mnemonic devices in traditional performances. Repetition is very important, as song lines are sung over and over with varying cadence in the song-cycles. In performance these can have a chorus effect called 'tracking'. When the lead singer has sung his or her line, and the voice is just dying away, the group of other singers comes in and repeats the line, and after they have finished the main singer takes up again.

Song-cycles are also likely to work with memory in that they progress nomadically, going from place to place across a stretch of country, literally following in the footsteps of the ancestor who first walked through there and created the landforms. Knowing the performance text thus means to also know the country, and what it has to offer in terms of water and game, as well in historical and spiritual significance. Formulaic repetitions and elaborations are also a feature of narrative, both traditional and modern. Paddy Roe (Muecke 1982, 204) uses cross-paralleled repetitions, which Homeric scholarship has taught me to recognise:

> 'we pull up under this tree' he say
> 'this tree we pull up
> we pull up under this tree'.

or these three lines which start with an inverted repetition and then elaborate (1983, 4):

> he come back from fishing
> got all the fish come back
> so he comeback on the other road.

Anybody could learn a lot about storytelling from Aboriginal narrators many of whose techniques are shared with any culture which maintains an oral tradition. It should be noted (in parenthesis) that storytelling is not given a high priority for arts funding in Australia, unless it is turned into something tangible like a film or a book.

Historically, what has happened to traditional texts is that they have been translated into English, and in the process shifted into whatever is seen as the most appropriate Western genre. Paraphrase was then the most important rewriting technique, as the social and ethical importance of the original stories and songs was stripped away in favour of some basic human or anthropomorphic content. Children's stories were seen as an appropriate destiny for the texts, and one traditional narrative device of (magical) transformation was retained for 'just so' type stories: how the echnida got her quills (having once been a woman) and so on. The use of Aboriginal children's stories in translation may be appropriate, but something much more serious is going on when major texts are reduced for this purpose.

A number of important works have been published in what I might come back to call traditional Aboriginal literature, because they have appeared in book form. There is the magnificent *Djanggawul* song-cycle translated by the Berndts in 1952—for which the original text is published elsewhere. There is Strehlow's *Songs of Central Australia* (1971) which was translated by one of the few Europeans to have been brought up speaking an Aboriginal language as well as his own. There are numerous other translations, some with extensive explanatory texts. All of them experience difficulties with the translation, and it could be said that a lot of these derive from the potential reader not knowing the country.

If one is familiar with the landforms, as well as the local flora and fauna, these texts would be much more accessible. Not only do the symbolic and practical significance of these things resonate throughout the texts, but people and things, in the mythological narratives undergo transformations (say from man to animal, or parts of the body radically changed) which make a realist reinterpretation or rewriting impossible.

The only way a traditional song-cycle like *Djanggawul* can be meaningfully and adequately performed is in its original setting. When it is translated and explained by the anthropologist, the aesthetic or performative dimension largely drops away, and we are left with one (social scientific) interpretation of what it is about. But this is certainly enough to give some idea of the rarity of the work, and it makes one wonder how it might be performed if it were to be adapted for the city.

Possibilities for readaption are partly made possible through a shift in literary theory. Critics are now defining literature precisely as reinscription, or the transformation of genres. Postmodernism, in particular, makes a virtue of pastiche and the juxtaposition of styles, different sorts of texts playing off each other. Literature is being defined less and less within the liberal humanist tradition of realist expression in which the writer is usually in the business of recording his or her experience, or the experience of a whole class, in a 'sensitive and mature' way. Now literary effects are generated as texts to challenge the limits imposed by genre, discourse and authorship. The fact that Aboriginal texts are not clearly oriented in terms of these categories makes them immediately interesting for postmodernist aesthetics.

Nevertheless, the production of Aboriginal writings takes place in the context of a whole series of representations which is being used to produce definitions of Australian culture and nation leading up to the Bicentennial year. I think that in this context the regional has to be asserted against the national; that the place marked out for Aboriginal culture (as timeless etc) will have to be contested once again; that constructions of Aboriginality will have to be deconstructed and reconstructed for specific political purposes.

Once again, Aboriginal verbal art will be judged on its performance. It has shown itself in the past to be flexible and dynamic, incorporating new materials, but also withholding old ones. Against the will to know which Western science and liberalism have launched against Aboriginal peoples—to subjugate by finding out about them—the people have practised strategic non-disclosure. Against a hypocritical liberationalist ideology: 'Express yourself freely and you too will be free', Aboriginal people have often preferred to remain free on their own terms. One of the major strategies whereby Aboriginal people have retained a value for their culture is silence, and the public/secret division.

And if this writer has not been able to tell a great deal about traditional verbal art, could it not be that he was never meant to be a producer or an interpreter of that material, and that it really only makes sense for him to tell things from where he stands—to tell his own story, as it were, as someone involved in the social and institutional practices of textual production, someone who can talk about how texts are used without necessarily having to interpret them (in a literary mode) or classify them (in a social scientific mode).

Now in spite of my careful negotiation of a situation in which Aboriginal people are involved in the Aboriginalisation of their institutions, I found that my right to work in this area was challenged (from the floor at the Conference on Black Literatures, Brisbane, June 1986). I made sure I had designated myself as 'informed scribe', yet I was told that I was not the 'author' of the texts that I had produced, the implication being I had appropriated someone else's right as author (Paddy Roe, or another Aboriginal scribe).

It seems to me that I already knew as I wrote the paper that the only Aboriginal response would be one which challenged my right to speak, which is also my right to listen, to move around, to speak at conferences, and so on. Even though I was talking only on my own terrain, the political and performance aspects of my own speech had led me into dangerous territory.

The relative legality of a discourse or speaking position is perhaps the central issue for an Aboriginal criticism. Aboriginal textual criticism is only occasionally hermeneutic or aesthetic. The papers, and response to papers, in *Aboriginal Writing Today* (1985) mostly take the form of a kind of legislative work, an active working through of people's rights in relation to texts within a literary formation conceived of as a political intervention in Australian literature.

Exegesis, therefore, is mostly absent, as it would seem to be in traditional societies. Margaret Clunies Ross (1983, 21) claims in relation to these societies that:

> Explicit exegesis is unlikely to develop much in societies...in which there is a major disjunction in the flow of information within the social group brought by the restriction of higher levels of knowledge to adult men and the introduction of initiation grades among the males.

Exegesis, she argues, is needed if the canonical text becomes incomprehensible through age, when words become archaic. Either the archaisms are tolerated as some kind of mystical element, or exegesis retains them through understanding, knowing what they mean—this knowing being achieved through specific Aboriginal techniques of textual commentary or 'initiation'.

We are still a long way from knowing what Aboriginal knowing might be about in relation to major Aboriginal texts. Western societies, which practise exegesis, or the infinite proliferation of commentary building up a kind of encrustation of secondary texts around the primary text, do so not by virtue of the fact that hierarchies of knowledge have been eliminated. Nor should the repetition of such practices as commentary have any necessary relation to general social structure, such as the presence or absence of hierarchies. Nor will the continued repetition of such practices as exegesis or commentary take 'us' any closer to the 'true meaning' of any Aboriginal texts. There are no necessary points of overlap between European and Aboriginal reading practices.

The practice of commentary is introduced as a training at specific sites in the education system, a system which encourages a 'hermeneutic of the self', a training in quasi-confessional commentary according to which subjects perform their moral adequacy under the benevolent eye of the teacher. The teacher almost becomes a friend who helps the pupil get to know himself or herself. The proliferation of this particular discursive mechanism cannot be seen in relation to any broader structure of society. It is not necessarily because we are a society of a certain sort (hierarchical or non-hierarchical) that we come to say we 'know' about our canonical texts as if that knowing were a natural outcome of the society.

The Aboriginal technique of repetition and bodily inscription is also one in which subjects are trained in relation to locally available materials and social arrangements. Subjects will learn to repeat certain stories and songs about a country over which they have 'the rights', at least 'rights' is how it gets translated into English—a phrase which also gets widely used in relation to land rights, citizenship rights and so on. It could be argued that Aboriginal criticism is political and legalistic by default; it has not 'learned' to depoliticise the aesthetic. This could be an advantage or a disadvantage, depending on how one stands in relation to a 'politics and literature' debate. Aboriginal literary rights are (as far as I know) policed in terms of correct custodianship as well as the textual form. Setting up a performance seems to involve getting the right people to play their parts, as well as debating the precise and correct form of the text. Knowing the tradition thus means being able to remember the text exactly and set up the appropriate personnel for its performance.

I have not suggested that the 'performance' mode of the Paddy Roe texts is in any way closer to this form of cultural reproduction because it is still a form of rewriting those situations and representing them in a book. Epistemologically, it takes language and speaking positions as the conventional enactments which secure various communicative effects. It deliberately moves away from a realist epistemology in which the text is absent as a category making up the event. The realist ethnographer is the knowing subject who makes available aspects of the world. Realism relates a consciousness to the world without the intervention of textuality and the meanings carried by various conventional structures like genre, discourse, the use of proper names, dialogue, and so on. The invisible realist text, however, could possibly be made visible, reappropriated and made readable once more in the current critical situation in which 'performance' has achieved a valued position.

52 Connections

References

Benterrak, K., Muecke, S. and Roe, P.
1984 Reading the Country: Introduction to Nomadology, Fremantle Arts Centre Press, Fremantle.

Berndt, C. and Berndt, R.
1951 Sexual Behaviour in Arnhem Land, Viking, New York.

Berndt, R.
1952 Djanggawul, Routledge and Kegan Paul, London.

Clifford, J. and Marcus, G. (eds)
1986 Writing Culture: The Poetics and Politics of Ethnography, University of California Press, Berkeley.

Clunies Ross, M.
1983 'Modes of Formal Performance in Societies Without Writing: The Case of Aboriginal Australia', Australian Aboriginal Studies, No 1, 20–27.

Davis, J. and Hodge, B. (eds)
1985 Aboriginal Writing Today, Australian Institute of Aboriginal Studies, Canberra.

Harney, B.
1962 Tales From the Aborigines, Rigby, Adelaide.

Johnson, C.
1985 'White Forms, Aboriginal Content', in J. Davis and B. Hodge (eds), Aboriginal Writing Today, Australian Institute of Aboriginal Studies, Canberra, pp. 21–33.

Muecke, S.
1982 Australian Aboriginal Narratives in English—A Study in Discourse Analysis, PhD, University of Western Australia.

Roe, P.
1983 Gularabulu: Stories from the West Kimberley, Fremantle Arts Centre Press, Fremantle.

Strehlow, T.G.H.
1947 Aranda Traditions, Melbourne University Press, Melbourne.
1971 Songs of Central Australia, Angus and Robertson, Sydney.

References

Benterrak, K., Muecke, S. and Roe, P.
1984 *Reading the Country: Introduction to Nomadology*, Fremantle Arts Centre Press, Fremantle.

Berndt, C. and Berndt, R.
1951 *Sexual Behaviour in Arnhem Land*, Viking, New York.

Berndt, R.
1952 *Djanggawul*, Routledge and Kegan Paul, London.

Clifford, J. and Marcus, G. (eds)
1986 *Writing Culture: The Poetics and Politics of Ethnography*, University of California Press, Berkeley.

Clunies Ross, M.
1983 'Modes of Formal Performance in Societies Without Writing: The Case of Aboriginal Australia', *Australian Aboriginal Studies*, No 1, 20–27.

Davis, J. and Hodge, B. (eds)
1985 *Aboriginal Writing Today*, Australian Institute of Aboriginal Studies, Canberra.

Harney, B.
1962 *Tales From the Aborigines*, Rigby, Adelaide.

Johnson, C.
1985 'White Forms, Aboriginal Content', in J. Davis and B. Hodge (eds), *Aboriginal Writing Today*, Australian Institute of Aboriginal Studies, Canberra, pp. 21–33.

Muecke, S.
1982 *Australian Aboriginal Narratives in English—A Study in Discourse Analysis*, PhD, University of Western Australia.

Roe, P.
1983 *Gularabulu: Stories from the West Kimberley*, Fremantle Arts Centre Press, Fremantle.

Strehlow, T.G.H.
1947 *Aranda Traditions*, Melbourne University Press, Melbourne.
1971 *Songs of Central Australia*, Angus and Robertson, Sydney.

'Fiction or Assumed Fiction': The Short Stories of Colin Johnson, Jack Davis and Archie Weller

Adam Shoemaker

There are many loose definitions in the world of literature and one of the most imprecise relates to the Aboriginal short story. As commentators such as Colin Johnson (1985, 25–27) have observed, the question of what separates a tale from a sketch, from a short story in any literature is difficult enough, but the issue is further complicated in black Australian writing by the temptation of white critics to invoke the term traditional for any story which is set in a period prior to the European invasion of 1788.

The artificial barrier surrounding traditional culture in Aboriginal Studies is as imposing as the black monolith of Stanley Kubrick's '2001: A Space Odyssey'—and is often equally mystifying. The equation proceeds something like this: traditional Aboriginal culture equals corroborees, nomadism, initiation rites, and also legendary tales. If a contemporary black Australian author writes a story with any of these trappings it is dismissed by many readers as a fable (if it appears sufficiently creative in European terms) or as oral history (if it seems predominantly documentary). Therefore the Aboriginal short story has been, up to this point in time, largely relegated to the two camps of juvenile fantasy and quasi-anthropological oral narrative.

I will argue in this Chapter that these trends confuse the meaning of much black Australian short fiction. As I see it, what is most important is that the Aboriginal short story is a lucid form of cross-cultural communication. As such, it can often surprise the non-Aboriginal reader with its frankness, its honesty and its sociopolitical commentary. The black Australian short story is therefore often 'assumed fiction'—as Johnson calls it—because it frequently portrays actual events, circumstances and people in a fictional framework; the framework is familiar to the Western reader but the subject matter, style and dialogue often are not. It is a combination of these factors which has given the most successful Aboriginal short stories such a persuasive feel of authenticity—an authenticity which often blurs the distinction between fact and fiction.

Perhaps in part because the definition of the Aboriginal short story has been such a problematic one, it was not until the Adelaide Festival of 1986 that the first collection of short stories written by an Aboriginal Australian was launched—Archie Weller's *Going Home* (1986). Why did it take so long for this to occur? After all, this was more than twenty years after the release of Kath Walker's first collection of poetry (*We Are Going*, 1964) and the publication of Colin Johnson's first novel (*Wild Cat Falling*, 1965) and eight years after the appearance in print of Robert Merritt's play *The Cake Man* (1978).

One can suggest a number of explanations: poetry and drama were literary genres more amenable to Aboriginal creative and political aspirations because of their immediacy when read or performed, and collections of short stories have until relatively recently been considered fairly marginal economic propositions for commercial publishers. However, surely the same could be said for books of verse, yet poetry is apparently the single most popular medium of creative writing for Aboriginal Australians to this day.

I suggest a third factor is that white critics, publishers and commentators have largely failed to obtain a fix on the Aboriginal short story: it has been either edited down for a children's market (see for example, the editorial treatment of Dick Roughsey's work), or has been considered to be an oral record of the Aboriginal past by many anthropologists (see for example, Strehlow's *Aranda Traditions*, 1947).

It is only in the past few years that the definitional divisions have begun to be eroded, notably by works such as Paddy Roe's *Gularabulu* (1983) which is simultaneously short story, oral narrative and 'trustori' (true story). The publication of Weller's collection of short stories represented a different breakthrough: for the first time, an Aboriginal writer was credited with the ability to produce a book of contemporary stories which skilfully reflected the current urban and semi-urban black Australian subculture.

There is quite a strong dichotomy in Weller's writing between the purer restorative atmosphere of the country and the oppressive, corrupting atmosphere of the city. Unfortunately, this has misled at least one critic into thinking that Weller's own views of race relations are equally cut and dried. For example, in a review which practically suffocates under the weight of its own cliches, LV Kepert (1986, 102) observes 'Archie Weller is an angry young Aboriginal. ...The vision of the noble savage can expect an indifferent reception from our greedy society but Weller's stories should allow us to see Redfern and Moree with more understanding.' If Kepert had read the book with more sensitivity, then it would have been clear that there are no 'noble savages'—who are a fiction of European society in the first place—anywhere in its pages. Second, to characterise Weller as 'angry' is to typecast and denigrate him in a way which does no justice at all to the subtlety of his writing. Finally, the emblem of Redfern and Moree which Kepert uses is noteworthy, for one of Weller's most memorable messages in *Going Home* is that black Australians are not just ghettoised, but are oppressed on an individual level everywhere as they try to join white society. Assumed fiction—or the picturing of the real in a semi-fictional framework—is one of his greatest strengths.

Perhaps the best way to illustrate this aspect of Weller's stories is to compare them with those of his predecessors, Jack Davis and Colin Johnson.

Although Davis has not published a collection of his short stories, throughout the 1970s many of them appeared in the pages of *Identity* magazine, some under the pseudonym of 'Jagardoo' or 'Jaygardoo'. These stories are uniformly economical and well written and, as in all of Davis's work, manage to bring the Aboriginal past alive in the present. Whether he is describing the conflict between violent white explorers and bush-dwelling blacks or the forced removal of Aboriginal children from their mothers by the Western Australian police, Davis is pointed, and often poignant. He has the ability to encapsulate a single episode or event in poetic style, without engaging in artifice, by piercing straight to the heart of the matter. For example, 'Pay Back' opens as follows (1974a, 28):

> Munda has been trailing the party of three whites since early morning. He hated them. Yet within this hate was a mixture of fear. There were reasons.

Reasons indeed, for Munda soon has salt forced down his throat by the three explorers in order to ensure that he will lead them to water. But treachery finds its brothers out, for the soak which Munda leads the Europeans to is no salvation (Davis 1974a, 28):

> It was Wargoton who felt the first sudden swordlike thrust of pain. Then agony struck Lorrest then Wicknell. Wargoton looked at his companions, eyes bulging. He gasped, 'Liles, that bloody Liles has been here before us. He's always trying to wipe out the blacks, the soak has been poisoned.' Even with the dying light in his eyes.

Davis's mastery of irony is equally evident in another short story, 'White Fantasy—Black Fact' in which the bigoted bus driver does not permit a group of Aborigines to board, and then respectable white motorists refuse to stop to aid the blacks when an eight year old Aboriginal girl is bitten by a snake. Those who do stop—and save Katey's life—are thirty bikies emblazoned with skulls and crossbones on their leathers. The implication that only another group of outcasts from white society can have a real affinity with black Australians is inescapable.

In probably his most moving story, 'Deaf Mute Mother' Davis (1974b, 33) becomes a very directly involved narrator:

> She could not scream, but as long as I live, I will remember the soul shuddering heart rending attempts she made to voice her anguish.

In this account of the abduction of an Aboriginal baby from her mother by the authorities, Davis crosses the imaginary dividing line to the extent that it is impossible to determine, as Colin Johnson (1985, 25) has put it, 'where fact leaves off and fiction begins'. In other words, without having studied any Aboriginal history or having interviewed any black Australians about their childhood, the reader feels that such stories are inescapably authentic. The violence (both mental and physical) which Davis describes is so persuasive, so forthright and so compelling that one is hard-pressed to doubt its veracity. In other words, these stories are authentic because Davis describes experiences in Australia which are so typically Aboriginal in a very plain, open and effective style. In the case of his stories, the primary characteristic that renders them distinctively black Australian is their content; the style is relatively neutral.

Colin Johnson, the first published Aboriginal novelist, has theorised about short fiction but has not frequently practised the craft. In fact, what is noteworthy about Johnson's writing in this genre, is that he has published stories which, unlike those of Davis, have no overt Aboriginal content whatsoever.

The most striking of these 'A Missionary Would I Have Been' revolves around a mystical, dark night of the soul experience in Darjeeling. The story, which is as remote from Aboriginal culture as the Indian subcontinent is from Australia, is a catalogue of spiritual opposites and incongruities—of faces 'too real to be real'. Perhaps best described as a search for meaning or purpose in life, the story abounds in lush female imagery (1975, 10):

> The misty hills lay like a woman—and the road ran, black and glistening, littered with fallen boulders and debris, between her thighs, to end in a rush of converging red.

The content of the story is literally overwhelmed by its imagistic and poetic style: 'Stillness of the early hours, neither morning nor night; stillness of the soul after its panic flight' (1975, 10). And, in another short story of that era, Johnson explores this concept of the panic flight even further. In 'Safe Delivery'—a patently ironic title—the author examines the psychological trauma of space travel in which the helpless voyager becomes increasingly paranoid (1976, 7):

> In terror, he could only huddle there waiting for the moment of *safe delivery* which, in itself, was becoming more and more a vagary.

As in the case of 'A Missionary Would I Have Been', the style of the story is paramount, for the detached, technical language mirrors the isolation of the protagonist. But again, the story is, both literally and figuratively, a million miles away from black Australia. It is, of course, somewhat unfair to Johnson to cast his early short fiction in this light, as it clearly represented stylistic experimentation. Moreover, he has in recent years begun to write stories which are reworkings of Aboriginal oral history and, as such, are indigenous both in style and orientation.

Nevertheless, these early stories were also written by a black Australian, so should they be considered any less authentic in Aboriginal terms than those of Davis? I would argue that, to the extent that style overrides meaning they should be—these stories are clearly fiction rather than assumed fiction. Although the issue is a contentious one, I suspect that Johnson himself would admit to being more at home with his recent short fiction than with his earlier work. Yet, being non-Aboriginal in subject matter, style and dialogue, those first stories provide a clear contrast with the writing of Davis and, to an even greater extent, with the stories of Archie Weller.

Weller was very impressed by Johnson's first novel, *Wild Cat Falling* (1965) and the influence of that book is clearly evident in Weller's first published short story, 'Dead Dingo' (1977). In fact, the first sentence of the latter is a paraphrase of the former; Weller writes (1977, 28): 'The gates close behind him and he's free. Free? Ha, that's a laugh.' Johnson's (1965, 3) opening line had been: 'Today the end and the gates will swing to eject me, alone and so-called free'. But the first impressions of Weller's style were deceptive for, rather than being derivative, he has since 1977 broken new ground both in the Aboriginal novel and in the black Australian short story. One of the key factors in this achievement is his remarkably sensitive treatment of dialogue. Weller has an uncannily keen ear for Nyoongah—the collective, contemporary Aboriginal language of the Perth area—and for the gutter speech of poor whites and other down-and-out groups. Even in 'Dead Dingo' this talent is apparent in Weller's catalogue of party talk (1977, 28):

> Wally Goyne 'ad a blue wiv a skin...caught th' clap off Annie...dough's run out, 'ave to do somethin' soon...aw, Josephine's turned lesbian, I reckon...so 'e got stuck on th' roof, when th' fuzz come they jus' took 'im...dobbed in fer sellin' smack...ten years fer rape.

This is vibrant, authentic dialogue in which style truly is meaning. In other words, in Weller's work, the subject matter, the style and dialogue are all typically Aboriginal and, for this reason, his short stories are even more distinctively black Australian than those of Jack Davis. At the same time, Weller has a keen perception of white speech patterns—especially those of the police—and these emerge most clearly in the recently, published collection *Going Home* (1986, 90):

> By Christ, you're in the shit now. Tell us who the others were, or we put everything on you. Hey, sarge, one went down along the river. Where'd that bloody girl go? I wouldn't mind arresting her, eh Billy?...Listen, Jacky, yer better start talkin' soon, before I belt yer bloody ears off...How's Mal? Pretty crook, that boong's got a hard punch. Yaaah! They all think they're Baby Cassius.

It is not merely the overpowering sense of veracity which marks Weller's short stories. It is also the oscillation in his work between the brutal and the lyrical, between action and reflection. For example, what is particularly memorable about the story, 'Herbie' is the delicate portrait of a small Aboriginal schoolchild. In the following passage what is implicit concerning ideology is as important as what is explicit concerning white prejudice (1986, 97):

> All Herbie wore, summer or winter, were a pair of dirty blue levis and an old T-shirt. Then one day he come to school in a new red-and-white check shirt. He was real proud of that shirt: we could see by the way he kept touching it with his hands, like it was a young rabbit, or fox, or bird, or something. Well, at break, us kids surrounded him and belted him up a bit, then I yanked him up off his feet and I said something like, 'This shirt's too good for a dirty black boong like you, so I reckon I'll have it.' Then I tore it off him and messed it up, then ripped it up and laughed into his face. He

cried a bit, but he was an Abo so didn't cry for long—he only hated me. I see now that it must have been the only absolutely new thing his family or anyone had ever given him.

This passage is an extremely rich one, and it relies for its richness upon much more than black Australian content per se. It is the Aboriginal attitude toward nature which is portrayed here, the viewpoint born of poverty, the stoic superficial acceptance and deeper resentment of prejudice, which all contribute to the creation of a distinctive black Australian atmosphere. Moreover, although the passage does not concern a specific sociopolitical issue (such as mining or land rights), the Aboriginal viewpoint is clear and impressive. It has perhaps more impact upon the reader than if Weller had been describing, for example, a political rally.

In summary, Weller's short stories are strengthened by his deft combination of a unique Aboriginal creole, a typical black Australian situation and a particularly effective and sensitive stylistic approach. It is the combination of these three factors which renders his fictional treatment of typical Aboriginal experiences, or assumed fiction, so successful.

It is remarkable that three of Australia's foremost Aboriginal short story writers have all come from the same area of the country (Western Australia), and that only one has so far published a collection of his short fiction. Yet, despite their shared geographical background, Davis, Johnson and Weller have all gone in different directions in their writing. Davis has looked to Aboriginal history in Western Australia for much of his inspiration, and his stories are marked more by typically black Australian circumstances than by a distinctive style of writing. Johnson, on the other hand, has engaged in wide-ranging stylistic experimentation in his stories which has taken him far from Aboriginal themes. While Davis has explored assumed fiction, Johnson has written pure fiction. Weller has also produced assumed fiction but, unlike either of his predecessors, he has avoided both the content-based and the experimental approach. Instead, he has married Aboriginal subject matter and dialogue with a distinctive black Australian style of writing to produce a successful synthesis.

All three authors have written authentic short stories in their own terms, but Weller seems to have achieved the most in terms of overall Aboriginal authenticity. So far, the Aboriginal short story has been rarely published, scarcely defined and even less frequently analysed. In the wake of Weller's success and as Aboriginal literature continues to grow, so may public and critical interest in black Australian short fiction, assumed or otherwise.

References

Chee, R.
1977 'Dead Dingo', *Identity*, January, 28–30.

Davis, J.
1974a 'Pay Back', *Identity*, January, 28.
1974b 'Deaf Mute Mother', *Identity*, April, 33–36.
1978 'White Fantasy—Black Fact', *Identity*, April, 27–29.

Johnson, C.
1965 *Wild Cat Falling*, Angus and Robertson, Sydney.
1975 'A Missionary Would I Have Been', *Westerly*, March, 9–14.
1976 'Safe Delivery', *Westerly*, June, 6–7.
1985 'White Forms, Aboriginal Content', in J. Davis and B. Hodge (eds), *Aboriginal Writing Today*, Australian Institute of Aboriginal Studies, Canberra.

Kepert, L.
1986 'A Rare Insight, From an Angry Young Aboriginal', *The Sun Herald*, 30 March 1986, 102.

Merritt, R.J.
1978 *The Cake Man*, Currency Press, Sydney.

Roe, P.
1983 *Gularabulu: Stories from the West Kimberley*, Fremantle Arts Centre Press, Fremantle.

Roughsey, D.
1971 *Moon and Rainbow*, A.W. Reed, Sydney.

Roughsey, D. and P. Trezise
1978 *The Quinkins*, Collins, Sydney.

Strehlow, T.G.H.
1947 *Aranda Traditions*, Melbourne University Press, Melbourne.

Walker, K.
1964 *We Are Going*, Jacaranda Press, Brisbane.

Weller, A. (see also Chee, R.)
1986 *Going Home*, Allen and Unwin, Sydney.

Black Literatures in the Pacific: The Spider and the Bee

Trevor James

Discourse about black literatures is valuable to the extent that it can provoke insights—but it becomes misleading when pressed too far. In the South Pacific, the particular experiences of Aboriginal, Maori and Oceanic writers cannot be subsumed adequately within the connotations of a package labelled 'black'. My intentions begin with the proposal that one way (I stress that this is only one way, because there can be no monopoly on critical response) of approaching the black literatures of the Pacific is through the relationship these literary works have with the cultural resources of black and white society. I also suggest that black American writing has been shaped by the physical absence of a cultural base and has had to create one, and that Aboriginal writing has had its indigenous cultural base so eroded that its writing appears increasingly to conform to white society. Finally, I suggest that the dominance of Maori writing in the black literatures of the Pacific owes much to the fortunate retention by Maori people of their own culture, and its ability to adapt to radical change.

I begin here despite the examples of Derrida, Barthes, Foucault, Lacan, and Kristeva, and despite the fashionable displacement of author, reader and meaning as central to criticism, and indeed despite all the giddy cerebrations of this post-Saussurean critical assault upon language and the idea of literature. I begin here because the human reality engaged in the 'new literatures' is otherwise demeaned. In these literatures, where the writer's person, social situation, and readership are shaped by acute forms of dispossession, such critical refinements are irrelevant if not even decadent. Here the critic must comprehend the formative reality from which a literature emerges, and adopt a critical approach which does not compound the experience of being dispossessed and the critic must be careful not to compound this. The writer's need to establish some personal 'order' over the chaos of experience, some standpoint or ground of being, from which he or she may formulate the experience of being black and yet living white, is fundamental. I believe the consistent allusions to the land and its traditions signifies the search for such a base. Ezekiel Mphahlele remarked to Sonia Sanchez (1977, 30) when he eventually returned to South Africa after voluntary exile:

> I must be buried in my country in my own homeland, my bones must replenish the black earth from whence it came, our bones must fertilize the

ground on which we walk or else we shall never walk as men and women in the 21st century.

Of course the question of where a writer starts from is not a new one. We can see this in Swift's prose satire on the dispute between the rival merits of ancient and modern learning, *The Battle of the Books*, which utilises an argument between a spider living in a corner of the library, and a bee which has got tangled in the spider's web. We are told that the spider is like the moderns who spin their writing out of their own entrails, while the bee is like the ancients who go to nature for their honey.

I propose to borrow the terms of Swift's satire for writers in the new English literatures, thus: on the one hand the bee, the nature of Swift's ancients, may signify the land and traditional society with its customs, and cosmology; on the other the spider, the moderns, may signify the metropolis of contemporary secularised Western society. Each of these opposed terms possesses a literature: the land's most natural expression is in an oral literature, and 'closed' texts; whereas the composite and complex reality of the metropolis tends to create 'open' texts. The Harlem Renaissance, and the emergence of a sophisticated black literature in South Africa, are examples of this. As far as the latter is concerned, Ezekiel Mphahlele (1967, 247) remarked at a conference on African literature in 1963, that:

> During these three centuries, we the Africans have been creating an urban culture out of the very conditions of insecurity, exile and agony. We have done this by integrating Africa and the West.

Yet, as I have indicated, there exists a tension between land and metropolis—both are modes of awareness which conflict with each other. VS Naipaul (1964, 228) discerns this in Indian literature, and suggests that in *The Rebel*, Camus expresses something of this conflict (which may point to the distinction between open and closed texts):

> It is possible to separate the literature of consent, which coincides by and large, with ancient history and the classical period, from the literature of rebellion, which begins in modern times. We note at the scarcity of fiction in the former. ...The novel is born at the same time as the spirit of rebellion and expresses, on the aesthetic plane, the same ambition.

The example of black American writing

Unlike blacks in South Africa, for American blacks the spider appears to have devoured the bee. They have lost a country of their own and have had to spin an identity from a common history of suffering. They have had to create an identity, find a home from which to write. That home has been established within the metropolis. So there is Harlem and the Harlem Renaissance; and today a substantial and sophisticated literature which boasts hundreds of writers.

But the search for a black home has been a long one. It precedes urbanisation. It begins in the experience of displacement that gave birth to the spirituals with their yearning for the land, a home. But home is somewhere else, never 'here'. So, in the spirituals the home is a heavenly one. There are numerous examples from the various song texts that can be found.

> Sometimes I feel like a motherless child,
> A long way from home...

> Swing low, swing chariot,
> Coming for to carry me home...

> I got a home in dat rock,
> Don't you see?...
> Poor man Laz'rus, poor as I,
> When he died he found a home on high,
> He had a home in dat rock,
> Don't you see?

> Deep river, my home is over Jordan.

> I am a poor pilgrim of sorrow...
> I'm tryin' to make heaven my home
> Sometimes I am tossed and driven.
> Sometimes I don't know where to roam.
> I've heard of a city called heaven.
> I've started to make it my home.

For some, heaven appears to have been abstract, and others have looked for a more tangible base. Black American culture has never quite forgotten the bee, and it has continued to refine the search for a home, for the land in which it may ground its being. It has looked to Africa. Richard A Long's (1972, 424) remarks on Africa are fairly representative. He speaks of Africa and the 'diachronic principle of the African continuum' in highly symbolic terms:

> The principle is, that historically radiating from the Black Core, the Black peoples of the world have carried with them modes of dealing with and symbolizing experience, modes discovered and refined through millenia in Africa itself, and that these tactical and symbolic modes constitute a viable nexus of Black culture, one of the major traditions of humanity.

Africa then is, as it were, 'in the heart'; it is the symbolic, if not the actual, ground of Black Being. The consequence of this is that black American writers have imaginatively reinstated the bee, symbolically fused land and metropolis. The attempt has been that they should secure the best of both worlds: Africa as their land, the repository of black identity; and their place in the metropolis, an assured achievement within the culture of the West.

Aboriginal writing

Of the literatures of the Pacific, Aboriginal and Maori writers have experiences which bear some resemblance to those of black Americans. Aboriginal writers appear very conscious of the influence of black American culture, and also torn between the claims of the spider and the bee. Estranged from the land, alienated in the metropolis, Aboriginal writers appear to lack a ground for their being from which they can speak, and are in the process of going—as Kath Walker's poem 'We Are Going' reminds us.

The present tense is important. Aboriginal writing shows scant evidence of any happy nostalgia for traditional life on the land. The memories of home are generally characterised by deprivation, racism and bitterness. With displacement such as they have endured, the literature is more concerned with conflicts that Maori writers have not had to face so acutely. Unlike Maori literature, there is no pastoral tradition as a major strand in the literature, the basis for it does not appear to exist. Instead, Aboriginal writing is about rediscovery, reclamation, retrieval and—ultimately—about survival.

Archie Weller has shown considerable talent in both the novel and short story genres. His recent collection of short stories, *Going Home* (1986), is an important achievement. Even the dust jacket is iconic of this quest: on the front cover is Fred Williams's painting 'The Steep Road', on the back is Drysdale's 'Man in a Landscape'. The one may signify a difficult progression toward an uncertain destination, the other—of an alienated Aboriginal figure in European dress limply touching the rocks of a desert landscape—carries heavy connotations of contradiction and estrangement.

In the title story, in fact on the first page, the protagonist (who has been assimilated within white Australian society) drives a sleek new car on the journey which provides the title for the collection. Yet the story has an ironic perspective, and the authorial presence is felt obliquely through the cassette of Charlie Pride singing 'I want to go home'; this is reinforced more overtly in the commentary which confronts the reader with a sense of black identity (1986, 1).

> The slender black hands swing the shiny black wheel around a corner. Blackness forms a unison of power.

In another story, 'Saturday Night and Sunday', which concerns the dilemma of two alienated Aboriginal boys who take part in a robbery, one reflection suggests that a black identity for Aborigines may be distinct from a wider black consciousness. At one point, one of the boys, ironically named Elvis, casts an envious and disillusioned glance at black America (1986, 63):

> Softly, disconsolately, hum a pop song. The negroes all have their spirituals and blues to keep them united. Elvis only has a white man's canned song to sing.

While it is easy to make too much of such textual slices, their recurrence is sufficient for the critic to take them very seriously. In the first, 'Blackness forms a unison of power', Weller presents an image of a wider identity: something not based upon a particular culture, or a place in society, or even the land, but an experience and awareness conveyed through differentiation, black opposed to white. 'Saturday Night and Sunday', with the contrast of Aboriginal Australians with black Americans, implies a further distinction—that Aborigines do not yet possess the cultural base that has been realised in black American culture.

The land in Aboriginal and Maori writing

The critic has to remember that there is one differentiation which has to be made between the experience of black Americans, and that of Maori and Aboriginal writers. For the latter the bee will not go away: they remain in the land of their ancestors physically, even though they may be displaced from ownership to greater or lesser degrees. They also remain aware of a traditional culture which draws its 'nectar' from the land. In that sense they have not been able to start afresh—they have been continually challenged by the rival claims of the bee, the traditional reality signified by the land, and those of the spider, the new order realised by the metropolis.

In such a situation the land and its traditions do not always assist the writer. Mphahlele (1967, 247) made the point that traditional culture can be used by white society as an instrument for perpetuating white dominance. It is not in the interests of that dominance that 'traditional' society should change.

> The bits of what the white ruling class calls 'Bantu culture' that we are being told to 'return to' are being used by that class to oppress us, to justify the Transkei and other Bantustans. And yet there still survive the toughest elements of African humanism which keep us together and supply the moral force which we need in a life that rejects us.

Sometimes—with disastrous consequences—Aborigines themselves may accept the idea of 'traditional' society as the basis of self-definition. In a controversial essay a West Indian writer and critic, the late Shiva Naipaul (1986, 19) identified such an understanding of Aboriginality as being a 'sublimated racism' and involving 'escape into an adventure playground of timelessness' which took no account of the reality of historical process. Or else, when the land and its traditions are still accessible to the writer (and this is by no means always the case), these traditions may not be accommodating to change. The values of the bee may be communal rather than individual; its interests may be preservation rather than adaptation. In a society which has a specific social context for its arts, literature as we know it may not belong.

On the positive side, where it can be accessed by the writer, there are nonetheless occasions when traditional culture provides precedents, concepts, ways of looking at the world, from which the writer can draw, even though the relationship with those traditions may be uneasy. On such occasions tradition and land provide the writer with the residue of a cultural base which, while not necessarily complete, may be enough to assist in the task of mediation between cultures, and in the business of helping to bring in the new.

To apply these general considerations to Aboriginal and Maori literatures is to indulge in further generalisations. As far as Aboriginal literature is concerned, although there are numerous collections of traditional tales, there appears little evidence that Aboriginal mythology has assisted Aboriginal writers in the business of mediating between the claims of the spider and the bee. Perhaps the mythology is more exclusive, the bee more intransigent.

On the contrary, Maori culture provides some evidence of being accommodating to new influences. Traditional *waiata* and *marae* etiquette, as well as aspects of fundamental mythology, have proven adaptable to new circumstances. Take, for example, the Maori mythology of the canoes which bring the people to New Zealand. This is central to Maori tradition, but it has proven capable of being inclusive rather than exclusive. The writer can recall being received onto a small *marae* on the Napier–Taupo road where, inside the meeting house, placed alongside those of the other ancestors, was a painted panel which clearly showed the landing of a uniformed gentleman in eighteenth century dress and a sailing ship. It was clearly meant to depict the arrival of Captain Cook. When complimented on their innovation, the elders explained that this was no innovation, and that when the *marae* had been restored, and panels cleared of paint which had been hastily put over them many years earlier, this panel was uncovered. They had merely restored what was already there. On *maraes* today Pakeha visitors may be told that they came late in the last canoe. This may be little more than a jesting courtesy, and the accommodation which *Maoritanga* may be prepared to make with Pakeha society can vary from place to place. Nonetheless, Maori mythology has been able to accommodate invasion, and the easy use Maori writers make of this mythology suggests that it has proven a help rather than a hindrance.

Maori writing: a place to stand

Fundamental to the way Maori people live is the idea of being *tangatawhenua*—that is to say local people, belonging to a place, and possessing a *turangawaewae*, which literally means 'a place to stand' and indicates that such a person holds speaking rights on a particular *marae*. The *marae* is a central institution in Maori society; it is a ceremonial centre dedicated to gatherings of Maori people, and *maraes*, some huge, elaborate and formal in their appearance, others, small and very simple, are a familiar sight throughout the New Zealand landscape.

The key concepts which I want to identify at this point are the sense of belonging to the land, and the sense of place and rights which flow from that. While these rights of *turangawaewae* are not inalienable but have to be worked at, the survival and vitality of these concepts today does much to explain the strength of Maori writing and what defines it from other black literatures. Despite various differences, Maori people have both retained a cultural identity that is essentially continuous with their most ancient pre-European traditions; and they have been relatively accessible to one another through propinquity and language. In short, the domain of the bee remains generally accessible to Maori writers: they have a ground for their being in tribal land, *marae*, *Maoritanga* and language, and these figure prominently in their works. Quite literally, the Maori writers have 'a place to stand' from which they continue to draw spiritual resources which contrast strongly with the expectations of the white critic. The poet Haare Williams (nd, 29), who

writes both in Maori and English, has eloquently expressed the Maori's tie
with the land in the poem 'Totara Tree'. Here the land speaks to the poet:

'At death
Body and soul are separated
Soul returns to the pito
The body to the land
Life born, is reborn
In the land'

With these words
The meaning came
Land is sacred
Communal
Eternal
Whoever understands its sacredness
Can never forget it
Nor violate it

To destroy it
Is to destroy a history
A people and a future

We planted
The totara tree
The ground freshly turned

Reminded us of a burial
Placing there part of us
Our umbilical link
With people and land—
Ancestors

Whereas black Americans may evoke an African continuum, the Maori
possess and inhabit a Maori continuum. Accurate though I believe this
description is, it is important not to produce an idealised scenario. During
the past 150 years of colonial settlement, there have been times when the
Pakeha spider almost digested the Maori bee! Early this century there was
a massive fall in the total Maori population; whole communities were
decimated by influenza—as can be seen in Maori cemeteries throughout the
country. Many Maori people drifted into the cities for work; *maraes* fell into
disrepair; old ways were forgotten; Maori language declined. Although
assimilation (the official policy of the New Zealand government at least
between the years 1935–60) has been largely resisted, there was a time when
it appeared that a specific Maori identity might virtually disappear.

Though bruised by colonialism, Maori culture, with its curious mix of
pragmatism and conservatism, survived. Under the inspiration of great
leaders such as Apirana Ngata (1874–1950) it adapted without assimilation.
In the 1960s and 1970s new groups and events forged a militant Maori
consciousness: for example, the young radical *Nga Tamatoa*, the Maori Land
March from Cape Reinga to Parliament House in Wellington in 1975—a
massive symbol of Maori consciousness in which the poets Hone Tuwhare

and Rowley Habib participated (and which is reflected in their works). In short Maori culture is alive, well and assertive.

The vitality of the values of the bee, despite the influence of the spider, remains because Maoris have never had their place to stand utterly removed. That place, the *marae*, has been the one place left to Maori people where their identity, the Maori language and traditions, were not threatened. It has remained a bastion for *Te Wairua Maori*—the Maori spirit. *Maraes* have been rebuilt, in fact in Northland, where some Maori communities have almost been depopulated by the pressure to move to Auckland for work, it is interesting to see how may *maraes* have been restored, and the extent to which there has been a significant return to the land by Maori development cooperatives. Most important, at least as a symbol of the way in which Maoris have made the spider learn to co-exist with the bee, has been the establishment throughout New Zealand of some urban *maraes*. This has been a bold step since a *marae* has always belonged to a particular group: the advantage has been that it has allowed urban Maoris to maintain something of their *Maoritanga* and its reaffirmation. As one scholar has noted (Salmond 1975, 82):

> As always, the *marae* follows the people, and increasingly the location for new *marae* is in the towns.

Maori writing

The development and shape of Maori writing reflects the process of mediation between the bee and the spider, the land and the metropolis, and the anthology *Into The World of Light* (1982) provides a map to the diversity and strengths of this literature.

First, one should consider the domain of the bee, which is a Maori culture itself. Maori language, and its oral literature, has been a key resource that is demonstrated in the *waiata* (songs), and poems of Maori orators such as Wiremu Kingi Kerekere, Arapeta Awatere, and Maori women such as Kohine Whakarua Ponika and Kumeroa Ngoingoi Pewhairangi. The flexibility of the language and its forms, their capacity to adjust to a new situation, is impressive. There are numerous instances of *waiata*, sung on the *maraes*, showing a synthesis of the traditional and the contemporary— or, if we like, again the bee adapting to the spider. In 1926 Sir Apirana Ngata composed a famous witty and ironic *waiata* called 'The Cream Song', to help persuade east coast tribes to participate in government sponsored land development schemes. Even the popular Maori action song that is staple diet for tourists who watch Maori concert parties is mainly an innovation (Mitcalfe 1974, 157).

> In its present form (it) was evolved by Sir Apirana Ngata and other leaders of the Young Maori Party, who, in this, as in so many other things, managed to blend Maori and Pakeha elements into new forms, neither purely Maori nor European, but reflecting the modern Maori situation, between the two cultures, partaking of both. ...Today, there are compositions...which look back to the pre-European past and ahead, to the best that the new world has

to offer. Audiences, performers, are more sophisticated. Out of the spindly manuka, a new forest is springing.

In the words of Ihimaera (1982, 49), 'The oral literature, up until the 1960s, was the means of cultural transmission and preservation...so that we were able to understand what we had been and what we were'.

Maori writers have also drawn upon traditional materials such as customs and beliefs, the relationship with the land and aspects of Maori history and experience. There are various examples of this. One from the Maori drama is Harry Dansey's *Te Raukura—The Feathers of the Albatross* which deals with Te Whiti o Rongomai and his experiments on the *marae* at Parihaka in the Taranaki. In the novel form, Pat Baker's *Behind the Tatooed Face* might be considered a type of historical romance which, while it delicately deals with episodes important in the history of his own tribe and ancestors, looks at pre-Pakeha Maori society with considerable realism.

Yet the process of mediation between the old and the new, the values of the land and those of the metropolis, has not been easy. Maori writers have been conscious of the losses endured by their people and their culture: the loss of land, diminution of traditions and language, occasions of discrimination. For the most part these writers are those who have been brought up in close contact with the Pakeha system, and have almost been absorbed by the spider. As an act of instinctual self-preservation some have turned back to the traditional values: drawing upon early memories. From this developed a literature of nostalgia, a 'pastoral' fiction which, despite understated protests, essentially evoked the values of Maori traditional, and therefore rural, society. Examples of this are obviously Ihimaera's first novel *Tangi* and most of the works included in the first anthology of Maori writing, that by Margaret Orbell, *Contemporary Maori Writing* (1970).

This was a process of cultural retrieval and affirmation, the realisation of a place to stand, which took *Maoritanga* from the *marae* into a literature in English, and created a literature which addressed both Maori and Pakeha readers. The gains of the pastoral tradition are obvious. What is noticeable is the way in which those Maori writers who have chosen to use an English medium, and had to develop within a European monocultural context, have progressively become more assured in their use of *Maoritanga*—particularly during the 1960s and 1970s. This can be seen in the development of the poets Alistair Campbell and Hone Tuwhare, while the new situation can be demonstrated by looking at the work of Keri Hulme (Ihimaera and Long 1982, 257–72) whose poetry is more specifically defined by use of Maori cosmology—something that would not have been practical for earlier Maori writers in an English idiom.

However, the second element, the domain of the spider, is important in the development of Maori writing. There may have been a danger that the pastoral tradition, with its celebration of a Maori past, and its rediscovery of the land and Maori culture, was almost a narcotic: for while it enabled Maori writers to develop the literature, it failed to engage the serious threat which a massive Maori urban, or, more accurately suburban, population represented to Maori culture. The cultural stereotype encouraged by the pastoral tradition, namely that the Maori were a happy, easy-going, people who lived in close harmony with the land, was at odds with the social realities experienced by many Maori families for whom the drift off the land had terminated in the metropolis. There, in such large state housing estates as those of Otara and Porirua, or in 'poorer' areas such as Wellington's Newtown, Maori families experienced massive social dislocation, were in the lower socioeconomic group, and liable to forms of discrimination. While some parents attempted to keep ties with the land by occasional journeys back to the *maraes*, their children generally grew up without either much experience of that resource, or knowledge of Maori language: some succeeded in the Pakeha world; more tended to drift to unskilled work; and some joined street gangs or did a spell in prison or borstal where Maori numbers were disproportionately high.

Anger and social tragedy are real enough. Take for example the poem 'Sad Joke on a Marae' by the young poet Apirana Taylor. The poem is an excellent example of how a poet can have a double vision and, in the manner of the spider, spin a poem from the pain of loss but contain that anguish within the communal foundation provided by the bee (1985, 521–22):

> Tihei Mauriora I called
> Kupe Paikea Te Kooti
> Rewi and Te Rauparaha
> I saw them
> grim death and wooden ghosts
> carved on the meeting house wall
>
> In the only Maori I knew
> I called
> *Tihei Mauriora*
> Above me the *tekoteko* raged
> He ripped his tongue from his mouth
> and threw it at my feet
>
> Then I spoke
> My name is Tu the freezing worker
> Ngati D.B. is my tribe
> the pub is my marae
> My fist is my taiaha
> Jail is my home
>
> *Tihei Mauriora* I cried
> They understood
> the *tekoteko* and the ghosts
> though I said nothing but
> *Tihei Mauriora*
> for that's all I knew

While not a major poem, this has force. The grief and despair which underlie the poem are not left as hopeless rage but, contained within the firm traditions of the *marae*, have the force of a directed energy. Three points need to be noted. First, that the poem is laced with irony. Its title is drawn from the level of colloquial Maori *marae* life where elders point with scorn at Maoris who do not know their *Maoritanga*, or their Maori language; such Maoris are a joke—but a sad one. Second, there is the social context of the poem which generates rage and anger: the fact of urban Maoris who are cut off from traditional life and form an itinerant manual labour force that is associated with drink (DB being Dominion Breweries), violence and imprisonment. Finally, there is the traditional context of the poem. The poem reflects the structure of traditional Maori oratory. It begins with a recital of ancestors—a heroic Maori past. Beyond that the structure of the formal speech, initiated by the call to listen, *Tihei Mauriora*, follows standard etiquette—the identification of one's name and place of origin. On the front of the meeting house are the elaborately carved barge boards which meet over the roof to form a gable apex. In many meeting houses this join is surmounted by a complete human figure, the *tekoteko*, which project above the gable apex as a finial. The *tekoteko* was usually named after an ancestor. That Taylor has the ancestor give the power of speech to the inarticulate narrator implies faith in the residual power of a Maori spirit. In short, the disinheritance of Maori people, however hurtful, has not been complete. A place to stand still remains.

Maori writers have acted to redress the situation. The change is crystallised in the contrast between the pastoral nostalgia of Ihimaera's first collection of short stories, *Pounamu, Pounamu*, and the urban milieu, the parables of conflict and epiphanies of consciousness, which dominate *The New Net Goes Fishing* (1977). Since the 1970s, a movement particularly noticeable in prose, has been the shift to a more austere social realism with criticism levelled against both Maori and Pakeha. This new urban orientation was naturally enriched by a consciousness of Black Power and other liberation movements from the 1960s onwards. However, few references suggest any continuity of interest between Maori writing and black literature. Probably the most uncompromising is set in a prison: this is Bruce Stewart's story 'Broken Arse' which has a Maori protagonist, named Tu, the name of the Maori war god, who epitomises a powerful, ruthless, affirmation of Black Power. Stewart began writing in 1974 when on parole from Wi Tako prison. The final lines suggest the conflict and bitterness which are central to the story (1982, 178).

> We could all feel the stomping. It was a slow, deliberate stomp, though there wasn't a sound. They were stomping their feet, swaying their bodies from side to side like a haka. They stomped. Broken arse, broken arse. You couldn't hear a sound. They looked so black, so ugly, so strong. Henry and Piggy Screw looked so pale, so weak, so broken. Tu rolled a large, slow smoke.

Ihimaera's contribution to Maori writing is so substantial that it is important to see how he treats the experience of the metropolis, and to what extent he explores black consciousness and affirms a Maori identity against a Pakeha culture. 'Clenched Fist' is one of a pair of stories which do this, and its two

Maori protagonists recur in both stories: George and Api provide emblems of two possible responses to Maori life in New Zealand. George's Pakeha name implies his assimilation within a Pakeha society; Api, in both name, speech and hairstyle, offers a Maori one. But he expresses this through the clenched fist salute which, at the time this story was written, was synonymous with black identity. The implication is that within the metropolis, where *Maoritanga* is most estranged and a separate Maori identity most difficult to maintain, a place to stand is sought through the idea of a worldwide black identity. Although this black identity may be drawn upon, one exchange suggests this to be a stage which has to be grown out of, and the American or African connotations dropped. Yet that reading is only one possibility, the method is dialectical and the text open to a plurality of readings. After all, George may be wrong. It is tempting for the Pakeha critic to impose his or her own reading (Ihimaera 1977, 38–40).

> George was quite used to Api's opinion of him. The wonder was they were still friends.
>
> Leave it? That's the sort of thinking which lost us our land to the white man. That's how he got it over on us blacks.
>
> We're not blacks, Api.
>
> No Api, George said. He's not white and we're not black. Damn you, can't you get that into that thick head of yours? We should be able to work these things out as Maori and pakeha. Those imported American terms you use don't relate to our situation. They're loaded words, loaded with a lot of anger and hate that just doesn't exist here.
>
> Why are you like this? What happened? Why are you so rabid?
>
> I discovered something you didn't, Api answered. That the world is split into black and white. The system might have accepted you but it didn't accept me. I'm not nice, not weak like you are. I saw myself being pushed into a corner and I had no option except to fight back. For survival, brother. Survival.
>
> Melodrama. But behind the dark glasses, agony of total commitment for black revival and conviction of belief in white guilt.

Ihimaera appears uneasy with this material. In both 'Clenched Fist' and 'Tent on the Home Ground' subtlety and depth have been overwhelmed by structure and characters which explore racial conflict. Both act as parables of that conflict, and of the understanding that can be achieved. In both, consciousness is raised: George comes finally to acknowledge racism, both black and white, and understand why Api is extreme. But Api too changes. Api disowns claims for exclusiveness, for 'Maori rights' and instead asserts an inclusiveness, that the struggle is for 'human rights'. When he does so it is interesting to note that Ihimaera (1977, 152) has George align himself with Api and enter the Maori tent embassy.

> From within the tent came the sound of a guitar, singing and laughter. The sounds did not seem aggressive at all. We're protesting for human rights.

The general thrust of these stories, and indeed of the poems, suggests that while there are parallels between Maori and black literatures, there is little inclination on the part of Maori writers to align themselves with black writing. Perhaps remoteness from the rest of the world has had a part to play in this, but equally, the strength and vitality of Maori culture has given them resources and an identity of their own. So far the general trend of Maori writing appears to be more interested in mediation between the spider and the bee, the metropolis and the land, the Pakeha and the Maori, than in assertion of the primacy of one over the other. The consistent theme throughout *The New Net Goes Fishing* is the question of how to mediate between both spider and bee, how to retain the old alongside the phenomena of the new so that a new cultural reality will emerge which allows free movement between both worlds. As the old man says in the final story of the collection, 'Return from Oz', 'There is still a need for...the best of both worlds' (Ihimaera 1977, 152).

References

Baker, P.
1975 *Behind The Tattooed Face*, Whatamongo Bay, Cape Catley.

Campbell, A.
1950 *Mine Eyes Dazzle*, Pegasus Press, Christchurch.
1963 *Sanctuary of Spirits*, Wai-te-ata Press, Wellington.
1964 *Wild Honey*, Oxford University Press, Wellington.
1967 *Blue Rain*, Wai-te-ata Press, Wellington.
1972 *Kapiti: Selected Poems, 1947–71*, Pegasus Press, Christchurch.
1975 *Dreams, Yellow Lions*, A. Taylor, Martinborough.

Dansey, H.
1974 *Te Raukura—The Feathers of the Albatross*, Longman Paul, Auckland.

Ihimaera, W.
1972 *Pounamu Pounamu*, Heinemann, Auckland.
1973 *Tangi*, Heinemann, Auckland.
1977 *The New Net Goes Fishing*, Heinemann, Auckland.
1982 'Maori Life and Literature: A Sensory Perception', *Turnbull Library Record*, XV, 49–53.

Ihimaera, W. and Long, R.A. (eds)
1982 *Into The World of Light*, Heinemann, Auckland.

Long, R.A.
1972 *New Black Voices*, New American Library, New York.

Mitcalfe, B.
1974 *Maori Poetry: The Singing Word*, Price Milburn, Victoria University Press, Wellington.

Mphahlele, E.
1967 *African Writing Today*, Penguin, Harmondsworth.

Naipaul, S.
1986 'Flight into Blackness', *An Unfinished Journey*, Hamish Hamilton, London, 11–21.

Naipaul, V.S.
1964 *An Area of Darkness*, Andre Deutsch, London.

Orbell, M.
1970 *Contemporary Maori Poetry*, A.H. and A.W. Reed, Wellington.

Salmond, A.
1975 *Hui: A Study of Maori Ceremonial Gatherings*, A.H. and A.W. Reed, Wellington.

Sanchez, S.
1977 'A Letter to Ezekiel Mphahlele', *The American Poetry Review*, September/October, 30–32.

Stewart, B.
1982 'Broken Arse', in W. Ihimaera and R.A. Long (eds), *Into the World of Light*, Heinemann, Auckland.

Taylor, A.
1985, 'Sad Joke on A Marae', in I. Wedde and H. McQueen (eds), *The Penguin Book of New Zealand Verse*, Penguin Books, Wellington.

Tuwhare, H.
1964 *No Ordinary Sun*, Paul, Auckland.
1972 *Sap-wood and Milk*, Caveman Press, Dunedin.
1974 *Something Nothing*, Caveman Press, Dunedin.
1982 *Year of the Dog*, John McIndoe, Dunedin.

Walker, K.
1964 *We Are Going*, Jacaranda Press, Brisbane.

Wedde, I. and McQueen, H. (eds)
1985 *The Penguin Book of New Zealand Verse*, Penguin Books, Wellington.

Weller, A.
1986 *Going Home*, Allen and Unwin, Sydney.

Williams, H.
nd *Karanga*, Coromandel Press, Coromandel.

Ingqumbo/The Wrath: An Analysis of a Translation

Daniel Kunene

AC Jordan was born in 1906 in Mbokothwana, South Africa, where he grew up fully immersed in Xhosa culture and traditions. He studied and taught at some of the institutions which feature in his novel, namely St Cuthberts, Lovedale and Fort Hare. He obtained the BA degree at Fort Hare in 1934, taught at Kroonstad Bantu High School from 1936 to 1944, during which time he obtained the MA degree (1942) by private study from the University of South Africa. He also wrote *Ingqumbo Yeminyanya* in that period.

In 1945 Jordan accepted a lectureship at Fort Hare, and from 1946 to 1960 he was lecturer in Bantu languages at the University of Cape Town. While there, he obtained the PhD degree (Cape Town) in 1956.

Among other things, Jordan was a Latin scholar and had studied the so-called classical cultures with emphasis on Greek mythology. He also specialised in English language and literature which he taught with great success at Kroonstad Bantu High School. For his MA, however, he chose to research African languages with Xhosa as his main area of concentration. His field work was largely undertaken in the Cape Province among, inter alia, the Baca, the Hlubi, the Mpondo and the Mpondomise peoples.

Published in 1940, *Ingqumbo* was very well received, being judged one of the best novels by any standard, and certainly the best African-language novel in southern Africa if not beyond.

Jordan left South Africa in 1961 and, after a spell in London, taught at the University of California at Los Angeles in 1962–63, and then joined the University of Wisconsin's Department of African Languages and Literature at its inception in 1963. Jordan died in October 1968 in Madison, Wisconsin, USA. His unpublished manuscripts included two Xhosa novels, '*Ookhetshe Babhazalele*' and '*Ulubhelu, Ndongana*', the latter described as a historical novel.

Jordan as author and self-translator

The present published translation of *Ingqumbo Yeminyanya* entitled *The Wrath of the Ancestors* is not the result of AC Jordan's first attempt at translating this book. He first produced a version which he then apparently put aside, presumably because he was not satisfied with it. His second attempt reflected a completely new attitude to the entire work, and he proceeded to introduce new characters, develop new directions in the story, new situations and relationships of characters both old and new. Furthermore this version had a clear mission to 'educate' the foreign reader into the complexities of Xhosa culture and manners. There was, therefore, a strong undercurrent of anthropological and/or political messages, veiled or revealed to varying degrees according to the exigencies of storytelling and the author/translator's own sensitivity. That version, which exists only in typescript, contains the following notation, by Professor Harold Scheub, who apparently typed the manuscript, which occurs quite deep into the story:

> This is as far as Professor Jordan got with his English translation of *Ingqumbo Yeminyanya* before his death. He was, to use his own word, 'fattening' the original Xhosa text, adding significant material to the original.

Referring to certain outstanding reworkings of the original, Scheub continues:

> It is not clear where Jordan was going with this part of the narrative, and he left no notes which might offer clues. I have therefore added to this unfinished manuscript the author's first English translation, a translation which more nearly approximates the original Xhosa text.

Scheub then warns that, given this, the reader should expect discrepancies in the ordering of certain events in the story.

The Wrath was published in 1980, twelve years after Jordan's death. It may therefore be assumed that there was a 'third hand' involved that did all the editing, selecting and reordering of segments from the existing translation drafts, the reading of proofs and so on. Also crucial is the time-lag between the publication of *Ingqumbo* in 1940 and the preparation of the translation drafts leading up to *The Wrath*, around the middle sixties. There are events and situations in this time period that must have had a tremendous influence on the author-turned-translator. Firstly, by the time the translation drafts were being prepared, much had happened in the politics of South Africa—the escalation of racial tensions, the intransigence of the white racist regime in South Africa, the violent confrontations of the liberation forces with the system, the interplay of tensions among the different political organisations all purporting to fight for the goal of liberation, and, above all, the ideological growth and change of perception on the part of the intellectuals of the liberation struggle, of which Jordan was an active member. Thus it is clear that the social dynamics prevailing during and between the two crucial periods in which *Ingqumbo* and the different translation drafts were being created, were such that it would be unrealistic to expect that Jordan would not have been affected by them. The translator's political commitments, ambivalences, uncertainties, and the urge to educate, are factors he must come to terms with and control, given his awareness of the fact that his translation addresses a much wider audience, including the whites of South Africa who constituted the *herrenvolk* or ruling class.

Secondly, there is this very question of a new audience. It is obvious that a writer writing for an audience with whom a common culture is shared, makes certain assumptions concerning the audience's knowledge and acceptance of the culture within which the work is created. Thus in the scene right at the beginning of *Ingqumbo*, where MaMiya, the lady of the homestead, arrives from the fields to find male visitors lounging on the grass in front of her courtyard and she first passes directly to the house and, among other things, removes the girdle from her skirt to lengthen it before going to greet the men (1940, 2), the Xhosa audience knows that it would be disrespectful of her to go to the men without first adjusting her dress like that. In *The Wrath* this action, namely *ukukhulula umfinyezo*, is translated with an explanatory phrase added: '...she undid her girdle to let down her skirt, *this being a sign of respect*' (1980, 4). The italicised phrase is not found in the original, but is added to the translation because it cannot be assumed that the 'foreign' reader would understand why she did that.

Whites in South Africa and elsewhere who, even with the best will in the world, might still misinterpret, misunderstand, and even entertain a superior attitude toward some of the customs of the Xhosa people, are the targets of the digressions and asides intended to educate them. This suggests that Jordan the translator, aware of this new audience, tried to confront such eventualities and lay them to rest in his translation. Being the proprietor of the original work he would almost certainly be inclined to take much greater liberties in his translation than would someone else. The Xhosa language, customs, traditions, religious beliefs and general world view, all combine together to form protective layers that need to be penetrated if the outsider is not only to be shown, but also to be educated.

Thirdly, and parallel to the perspective of time, there is also the perspective of spatial distance, including exposure to a different culture. By the time Jordan started working on at least one of the translation versions of his book, he had been living in exile in the United States for no less than five years. This must have also affected his perception of society, and added 'the American' as another important dimension of his foreign audience.

It is clear that by the time he worked on his translation, Jordan had a lot more to communicate it to. The question can now be asked: How can a translator be loyal to the original work while insinuating other messages into it which the original did not have? There is, after all, the alternative to write another book altogether, in English, that would reflect his ideological growth, thus giving the original work a chance to be revealed to foreign audiences in translation approximating it as nearly as possible.

It must also be borne in mind that the creative artist in Jordan was always very self-assertive. It is my perception that this creative urge always forced its way into Jordan's translations, making them perhaps a little too 'free' and less faithful to the original than might be desired.

Another interference might have arisen from Jordan's changed attitude to the idea of literary excellence. I think there are indications in the translation that some changes were introduced with the intention of 'improving' the original purely from an artistic point of view. This, in turn, would have been reinforced by the awareness that the work was going to be judged by a wider, and likely more critical, audience.

Language and idiom

The linguistic and cultural difference between Xhosa and English is a veritable gulf which constitutes a tremendous challenge to the translator. The lexicon itself is more problematic than may be apparent to many people. The very concept of 'word' is one that has not been finally resolved by linguists, even for languages as close as Xhosa and Zulu. If one is a disjunctivist one will get more words per line than if one were a conjunctivist. A conjunctively written word will translate into several words in the target language. Morphology is therefore an aspect of the original language that must affect the translation. Syntax also plays its part in bedeviling the issue— just one more headache for the translator.

We leave for very last, the question of idiom. Anyone who has taught his or her language to foreigners will not have escaped the totally unreasonable question from students: 'Why can't we say...' followed by a string of words which 'translate' correctly, but make a totally unacceptable noise to the native. The student is concerned with individual words and their surface denotations, a translation of sorts. The poor teacher is hard put to explain that there are intangibles in the language which cannot be quantified or objectified as lexical items, where stringing words together might not only be useless, but sometimes positively dangerous. Every translator has to cope with that.

A classic example of the above problem that also serves as our entry into a detailed study of Jordan's translation, occurs in *Ingqumbo* in the scene where Ngubengwe, a Xhosa character, and Father Williams, an English missionary working among the Xhosa, are just leaving the village of Jenca. Jenca is a very traditional village whose residents are sometimes referred to as 'red-ochre' people. Because of the existing political crisis among Mpondomise, Father Williams and Ngubengwe have not been welcomed at Jenca. In fact the villagers have been distinctly hostile, and the headman refused to see the visitors. Any little mistake on their part could cost them their lives. Such a mistake does occur. Five young men from the village come toward them singing a song which to Father Williams signifies no more than the African's traditional love for singing, but which the narrator characterises as *ukuguya*—to engage in a song-dance in preparation for war. Ngubengwe, aware of the seriousness of the situation, warns Father Williams that they are in danger and should retreat, but the missionary pays no heed to his warning and they urge their horses forward. Ngubengwe and the narrator share the Xhosa culture, and therefore for them the scene they are witnessing is captured by the one terrible word *ukuguya*. In *The Wrath* (1980, 235) the translator resorts to descriptive phrases:

> Five strongly built young men suddenly left the drinking party, half-dancing, half-prancing with a running, rhythmic movement, past the headman's house and along the road leading to St Cuthbert's.

'Half-dancing, half-prancing, with a running, rhythmic movement'—all that to convey the sense of one word *ukuguya*. This simply underscores the fact that this action was totally outside Father Williams's culture and beyond his understanding. But he rejects Ngubengwe's translation and prefers his own superficial one. Next, one of the young men shouts at them and accosts them with a seemingly innocent request for some tobacco. The narrator of *Ingqumbo* (1940, 216, my translation) goes on to explain that:

> He (Father Williams) was accustomed to seeing black people enquiring about each other's health and sharing tobacco when they met on the road, and he thought that this request for tobacco was always a sign of friendship and good will. Little did he realize that sometimes a black man ostensibly asks for tobacco when in fact his intention is to insult the person he is asking.

Ngubengwe, on the other hand, understands both the words and their deeper significance, and thus realises the seriousness of the situation. Once again he warns Father Williams and at the same time remonstrates with the young man for his bad manners. The missionary again understands only the words, and, far from heeding Ngubengwe's warning, chides him for his 'unkindness' and proceeds toward the young men 'to give them some tobacco'—another tragic act of 'mistranslation'. The young men attack them and Ngubengwe is mortally wounded and dies later in a hospital. Father Williams, who has meanwhile been thrown from his horse, is saved by a village woman who rushes to the scene screaming and throws herself over him.

> The narrator of *Ingqumbo* (1940, 216, emphasis added) tells the reader in a short, tragically ironic statement: '*Ngelishwa* uFather Williams wayesazi isiXhosa', which means '*Unfortunately* Father Williams knew Xhosa' (my translation). In *The Wrath* (1980, 236, emphasis added), the translator tags on an explanatory phrase to underscore the irony of the statement. He renders it: 'Unfortunately Father Williams could understand the Xhosa language, *or at least he thought he could*'.

Father Williams's translation of *ukuguya* is 'The natives are happy'; Ngubengwe's is 'These young men are angry and ready to fight'. Father Williams's translation of *ndincazele* is 'Give me some tobacco'; Ngubengwe's is 'I dare you to carry my insult with you or fight'. If the theme of *Ingqumbo Yeminyanya* is seen by some as being a clash of cultures, this tragic scene is a poignant example of that. Father Williams understood the words, but missed the deeper cultural codings that were added to them for this particular occasion. These were fully understood by Ngubengwe whose knowledge of Xhosa went beyond superficial lexical meanings and turned words into objects or guideposts that point to the real meanings intended.

Translator's changes

When we talk about the 'changes' a translator makes, the underlying assumption is that there exist, between the two languages, certain areas of one-to-one relationships of vocabulary and idiom where the translator does not have to 'change' the original, since he can take advantage of these parallel relationships. If, in such a situation, he ignores these coincidences and contrives something different, then he is effecting a change. Such a change is voluntary or unforced. It is made for any one of a number of reasons including personal preference, a sense that the change improves the translation, to humour the foreign audience, and so on. That is where the question of loyalty to the original becomes a factor in evaluating the translation.

On the other hand, there are forced changes where no happy coincidences of vocabulary and idiom exist and the translator has to resort to searching and screening for the closest possible equivalents. Naturally, the Jordan translation shares all these problems.

While there are undoubtedly moments of high achievement in this translation, it is unfortunately true that many unforced changes have been made for reasons that are sometimes obvious and sometimes obscure. This makes for a lack of consistency of tone. If I tend to dwell on the negative side of Jordan's translation, it is largely because of the high esteem in which I hold his original work. This is the irony and the predicament I find myself in as a critic. I feel that a translation worthy of the power and authority of *Ingqumbo Yeminyanya* is still to be written.

Uncompensated excisions

Without counting any excisions of less than four lines, we still come up with approximately 330 lines of *Ingqumbo* omitted from *The Wrath*. Counting everything, we have the reader of *The Wrath* deprived of no less than 400 lines of the original story. Besides, since the excisions are made at different parts of the story, there are some problems of textual discontinuity. Some of the longer exclusions include the following: a twenty line paragraph from pages 7–8 of *Ingqumbo* (*The Wrath*, 10); sixty-six lines from pages 30–32 (*The Wrath*, 32); sixteen lines from pages 123–24 (*The Wrath*, 129); fifty-six lines from pages 168–69 (*The Wrath*, 178); thirty lines from pages 234–35 (*The Wrath*, 260).

There seems to be no artistic justification for the above, as well as other exclusions. On the contrary, there are situations where the omissions are quite clearly detrimental to the artistic integrity of the work. For example, the one-and-three-quarter page passage where Mphuthumi recalls his first meeting with Zwelinzima on the train many years before as he (Mphuthumi) was on his first trip to Lovedale as a student teacher, and how Zwelinzima, the veteran Lovedale student, took to him, and how their friendship grew from that day on, serves to link the past to the present. These thoughts are coursing through Mphuthumi's mind years later as he waits for Zwelinzima at their favourite meeting spot away from the college grounds, to tell him that he knows his identity as King of the Mpondomise people, and that a group of loyal Mpondomise, including Mphuthumi himself, are preparing for his secret return.

One other example of artistic merit of an omitted passage comprises the eight line paragraph concluding the scene of Zwelinzima's installation as king. It tells of the eloquent speeches made by people such as Dabula and Dingindawo, and concludes by turning the spotlight on Mthunzini and Mphuthumi who are sitting next to each other. The narrator states that, for different reasons, these two were not upset that the roles they played in Zwelinzima's return were not mentioned by any of the speakers. This reference recalls in the reader's mind Mphuthumi's strenuous efforts to facilitate the exiled king's secret return, and Mthunzini's secret but equally determined attempt to prevent it. To compound the irony, Mphuthumi, who still considers Mthunzini to be his friend, remains ignorant of the latter's acts of betrayal. Further, the roles to be played by these two in Zwelinzima's future, which Dingindawo is planning to sabotage, make their recognition by the narrator artistically very important, if not indispensable. Their physical proximity to each other in these circumstances is a strong statement in itself.

Reordering of chapters

One of the most disconcerting things about this translation is the reordering of chapters which makes it difficult for the reader to identify exactly where he is in comparing the two books. Fortunately the book is divided into several sections (Books) and therefore the disparity caused by the reorganisation of chapters is never carried over beyond the end of the book in which it occurs.

In Book I, Chapter 2 of the original is merged with Chapter 1 of the translation. Chapters 3, 4 and 5 of the original are then run together as part of Chapter 2 of the translation. That means that Book I has eight chapters in *Ingqumbo* and only five chapters in *The Wrath*. In Book III, Chapters 1 and 2 are run together as Chapter 1 of the translation, while 6 and 7 are together incorporated into Chapter 5. Here the original ends with Chapter 8 while the translation ends with Chapter 6. Book IV merges Chapters 10 and 11 into Chapter 10 of the translation.

If nothing else, this apparently idiosyncratic revision of beginnings and endings of chapters creates an unnecessary hardship and annoyance for the comparative reader.

References to reader (alias narratee) deleted

Some decisions are obviously not easy for the self-translating author. References to the reader, which are used liberally in the Xhosa have been carefully deleted from the translation. Did the author/translator find them cumbersome in the English? Did he find them awkward in the Xhosa original as he revisited the book twenty to twenty-five years later? Would he have avoided them if he had been writing *Ingqumbo* from scratch in 1960–65? In other words, had he revised his ideas of literary excellence in the last quarter of a century since the original work was written? From these questions and considerations it is clear that a self-translating author confronts us with a gigantic problem which we are spared if the work is translated by someone else. Proprietorship, propriety and ethics become a tangled mess from which we cannot hope to extricate ourselves.

Omission of honorific addresses

One of the most cherished values in the society within which the story of *Ingqumbo* unfolds is that of overt respect of an older person by a younger. That is why the little girl sent by Nomvuyo (older than she) to call Thembeka (older than she) says to the latter (1940, 19, emphasis added): '*Sis*' Thembeka, uya bizwa ngu*Sis*' Nomvuyo' ('*Sis*' Thembeka, you are wanted by *Sis*' Nomvuyo'). When asked whether Nomvuyo is alone, she answers that she is with '*bhuti* Mphuthumi', the honorific bhuti indicating that the young man Mphuthumi is older than the little girl. In *The Wrath*, the translator has consistently deleted these honorific titles, making the girl sound very rude indeed.

Compensated omissions and problem of hiatus

So far we have dealt with uncompensated excisions. There is, however, one very important part of the plot where the translator has engaged in a very bold recreation of the story which is substituted for the original. The rewriting occurs as the story moves towards its climax with the unannounced return of the queen, Nobantu, to the Royal Place at Ntshiqo. Since Nobantu threw the nation into a crisis by killing the sacred snake, the *inkwakhwa*, she has been living in forced exile at her parents' home at Mjika, on the advice of her husband's cousin, Vukuzumbethe. The Mpondomise have been outraged by her lack of respect for the traditional values they hold so dear, and irked to the end of their tolerance by her husband's misguided reforms. They demand that he marry a traditional wife who will be their 'Mother' in the same way that Nobantu is the 'Mother' of the educated Mpondomise, many of whom are naturalised refugees from Emboland, and are now known as the Mfengu. She and the king are going through the most difficult time as they try to cope with the stresses of their official and private lives.

When Nobantu cannot stand the separation any longer, she sneaks away from Mjika to return on foot to the Royal Place, carrying her child on her back. She has lost much weight, and is showing signs of incipient madness.

The manner of their reunion is completely reworked in the translation. In both the original and the translation, Vukuzumbethe, who very much loves his cousin, Zwelinzima, is on horseback returning from town when he sees Nobantu whom he hardly recognises at first. He relieves her of the child, and they walk together till they reach the Royal Place. But here *Ingqumbo* and *The Wrath* part company. In *Ingqumbo*, Nobantu finds Zwelinzima outside. He is so startled when he sees her that all he can say is 'But Thembeka, where are you going?', and he turns around and leaves. From then on Zwelinzima daily wanders in the open fields, sometimes not even returning home at night. Nobantu, on the other hand, does not talk to any one, and spends most of her time lying listless on her bed and staring blankly.

Things drag on from day to day till she becomes totally insane and ends up committing suicide by jumping into the flooded Bedlana River with her child in her arms.

In the translation Nobantu arrives at the Royal Place in Zwelinzima's absence and Vukuzumbethe gives instructions for her to be made comfortable. Meanwhile he intercepts Zwelinzima as he returns home in the late afternoon and leads him into the Royal Place by a side door. Over supper, he gently nudges the conversation toward revealing Nobantu's return. When it eventually becomes obvious to Zwelinzima that she and the child are actually back, he stands up excitedly and goes to the room where the two of them are sleeping. The reunion is a tender scene in which he fondly strokes and kisses her, picks up the child and hugs him, and then sleeps in another bed in the same room.

Next morning father, mother and son are all happily reunited, though it is clear that the mother is not well. Vukuzumbethe suggests that they get a doctor for her. Meanwhile he has already ridden through the night to go and tell Nobantu's parents her whereabouts so they should stop worrying.

A major problem that arises from this is that Jordan died before he could develop this recreation of the story in whatever direction he might have had in mind. Unfortunately when the translation manuscript was prepared for publication, no one noticed that the old chapter from *Ingqumbo* that followed the rewritten one in *The Wrath* now made absolutely no sense. Being meant to follow the reunion as told in *Ingqumbo*, this chapter makes several references to Nobantu's unconcern about her husband's whereabouts. He in turn is depicted as avoiding her and avoiding to come home, which puzzles everybody, including Vukuzumbethe. The latter eventually confronts his cousin who declares himself unfit to so much as touch Nobantu's hand since he has dishonoured their marriage vows by yielding to the pressure to marry another woman, though at this point this has not yet happened. We are told (1980, 259):

> That night the Chief again did not sleep in his house. And when morning came Nobantu did not seek to know where her husband was.

By this time more than a week has passed since her return, and this is the morning on which she sees the cattle driven out of the village to go and marry the 'traditional' wife for her husband, and she goes off her mind completely.

These are two different stories, and one wonders why this glaring disharmony of these renderings escaped not only the compilers of the manuscript, but also the publisher's readers and editors.

Deletion of conjunctions

Humble as they may seem, conjunctions reveal to us in a constant manner as the story unfolds, the changing patterns of the narrator's relationship to the material of his story, the concessions he makes, the reservations and misgivings he may have, his judgement of the relative importance of the story's elements, and so on. Or these may be reflections of a character rather than the narrator, if the story is being seen through his eye. Many conjunctions found in *Ingqumbo* are dropped from *The Wrath*. While it is true that the translator is often forced by the sheer disparity between the languages he is working with, to either join shorter sentences or break longer ones into several shorter ones, it is equally true that many omissions of conjunctions from *The Wrath* are voluntary. This unnecessarily distorts the relationships of the main and subsidiary or subordinate ideas as found in the original. However, the translator has to be complimented for the manner in which he has handled some of the more difficult, and more typically Xhosa, conjunctions. Such conjunctions as *kambe, kaloku, noko* and *kanti*, while easy enough to translate into kindred languages like Zulu, Swazi, Ndebele and even Sesotho and Setswana, are the translator's nightmare if the target language is, say, English. Jordan has handled these situations extremely well. An important function of these conjunctions is to reflect the narrator's close relationship with the logic of the story. For example, *kanti* generally introduces the notion that information hitherto hidden from a character is now being revealed. The narrator (and maybe the reader) has known it all along. The removal of the veil of ignorance from the character, all of which is cleverly manipulated by the narrator, is often signalled by *kanti*.

Inviolability of original work

I consider a published work to have a certain sacredness, an inviolability which a translator ought to respect. I contend that regardless of whether or not a work is translated by its own author, we should continue to regard the author of the original work and its translator as two separate individuals pursuing two entirely different tasks. By this token, I would consider it both proper and indeed a scholarly duty to separate Jordan the author of *Ingqumbo* from Jordan the translator who produced *The Wrath*. I would say that *Ingqumbo* is an excellent Xhosa novel, and *The Wrath* an English translation that does not do justice to that excellence.

I am aware that proprietorship will always prevail over propriety. It is not a legal question, but an ethical one. I am aware also that a writer never considers anything he has written to be beyond improvement. Indeed, that sometimes a writer looks back and regrets, rather helplessly, why he said certain things, or said them the way he did. The temptation to improve will always be there. Marilyn Gaddis Rose (1981, 3–4) has said that 'writers who translate their own works regularly take more liberties than another translator would'. Rose (1981, 6) also tells us that Barbara Reich Gluck 'claims that Beckett writes his first "draft" in French and translates it into English for the definitive version'. But where does this leave the critic? I would take the position that, if I can justifiably criticise Chris Swanepoel's translation of Thomas Mofolo's *Chaka* (Kunene 1981) into Afrikaans on the grounds that he has treated the author of the original with disrespect by leaving out chunks of the story without any explanation, then I should be free to criticise Jordan the translator with the same degree of candour.

Secondly, I would suggest that a translator must first and foremost feel a strong sense of loyalty to the original work, and must feel the need to respect and preserve its integrity to the best of his/her ability. It must constantly be asked whether the author of the original work would agree that the translator was representing the author well. It should be imagined that a bilingual reader may pick up the translation and compare it with the original. Would such a competent reader judge the translator as one who knows the language and culture of the original work? In other words the task must be approached with a sense of awe.

Since a translator is a self-appointed cultural go-between who voluntarily offers good services to make a work accessible to another cultural-linguistic group, it is incumbent on him or her to have both the loyalty and the competence. The translator must be conscious of the expectations generated in the readers of the translation, namely that, through it, they are going to 'read' the original work. That is why a translation continues to bear the name of the original author.

Linguistic competence is not enough. The translator must be both bilingual and bicultural and should have a sensitivity for the subtleties of both cultures. We now demand a second loyalty. After paying due loyalty to the original, the translator must then examine the crude work and imagine how it sounds to the ear for which it is intended. If the process has been truly loyal to the original, the present draft will sound terrible. The process of smoothing out the crudities of this first draft is, in fact, a process of compromise. It is an admission that the ultimate success of a translation depends on taking a little and giving a little on both sides (Johnson 1985, 143). This is not as easy as it sounds. Indeed some translations are marred by the translator's inability to maintain a reasonable balance between the pressures and demands of the two language/culture environments that are being harmonised. *The Wrath* is not exempt from this shortcoming. But then I should add that the chances for this unevenness are much greater where, as in *Ingqumbo/The Wrath*, the translator (a black South African) has had an intense political/social relationship with the speakers of the target language, a relationship demanding that the black should justify his very existence. This question is usually outside the scope of translation discussions. I am suggesting that in circumstances such as the ones referred to here, it is not only relevant, but urgent. Thus, what in other circumstances might be criticised on artistic grounds as exoticism or pandering to a foreign audience, must be seen here as an emotional reaction to generations of degradation. This statement is intended to explain, not to justify.

But as a third requirement, I would like to invoke the concept of forced versus unforced, or voluntary changes of the original. As a matter of principle, I would insist that a translator should not permit the luxury of unforced changes. The moment this liberty is taken, the translator is putting into doubt loyalty to the original author's work.

Given these constraints, there will still be differences between any two translations of the same work. But the differences will be ones that the two translators can argue about, each advancing reasons for the choices made. This is a very fruitful exercise, bound to enrich the perception of the two languages by those involved, for the benefit of all. This is the kind of difference that must be encouraged rather than discouraged. It is encapsulated neatly by Ross's (1981, 17) concept of the 'many-one relation' between the original and an infinite number of possible translations. He states that 'no criteria exist for distinguishing which of many competing translations is correct'.

On this note we may now bring this discussion to a close by looking in a comprehensive way at both *Ingqumbo* and *The Wrath*, and trying to find the essential Jordan in both works. Prior to writing *Ingqumbo*, Jordan had the emotionally intense experience of witnessing the burial of a Mpondomise king. The body was tied to a tree on the banks of a river chosen for this purpose. The tree was then ceremonially pushed over so that it fell into the river, pulling the body down to the bottom with its weight. That was the birth of *Ingqumbo*. Yet the book's purpose was not to instruct its readers about this or any other custom of the Mpondomise people, but to involve them in a dramatic representation and re-presentation of this tradition, woven around the tensions of the rivalry for a kingship which was complicated by a rivalry over a girl. *Ingqumbo* must owe its brilliance partly to its freedom from the requirement to instruct.

The Wrath, while also having moments of high achievement which show Jordan to be a master of the English language, is encumbered by the extra duty to instruct a foreign audience that is to varying degrees hostile and reluctant. It reflects the torment of a mind trying to restore a human dignity seriously outraged on both the personal and the national levels. Whether the instructional element expresses itself in 'explaining' Xhosa customs, making a political statement as in translating 'um-India' (an Indian) as 'Indo-African', applying new literary canons that are perceived as 'lacking' in the original, its effect is to divert the translator's attention from his principal concern by pressuring him to insinuate these new messages into his translation.

Yet even in this translation as it now stands, Jordan now and again treats the reader to a taste of his superior talent as a writer. The passage below is an example of the poetic heights that are sometimes reached in the translation. It occurs close to the end as the narrator contemplates Zwelinzima's brief, hectic and tragic life. It is a kind of epitaph, and I reproduce it both in the original and as translated in *The Wrath*:

> Wadlula ke uLangaliyakhanya. Ilanga elikhanyise okwemini enye kwelasemaMpondomiseni se libuye laya kusithela. Wayihamba indlela ayivulelwa ngamakroti akowabo—ayivulelwa nguNgubengwe noJongilanga.

Wadlula eselula—ngokwenkwenkwezi elukhanyo belukade lungaqondwa, ethe ngobusuku obuzukileyo, xa iinkwenkwezi zibalaselayo zonke ngokubengezela, yacanda isibhakabhaka, yatsho ngobuqaqawuli obugqitha zonke ezinye iinkwenkwezi, kanti se isiya kutshona okokugqibela ukuba ingasayi kuze iphinde ibonwe, ilishiya ihlabathi likhwankqisiwe, lineenkumbulo nokulangazelela, lingavumi ukuncama ukuba yoza iphinde ibonakale (1940, 249).

And so passed Langaliyakhanya, the Shining Sun. The sun that shone over the land of the Mpondomise for a single day had again sunk and gone. Zwelinzima had followed the path laid open for him by the heroes of the land of his fathers, laid open by Ngubengwe and Jongilanga. He died young, like a star, hitherto unnoticed, that on some glorious night, when all stars shine in splendour, cleaves the sky, excelling all the other stars in its dazzling brightness, only to vanish, never to be seen again, leaving the world wrapt in wonder, full of memories and longings, unwilling to despair of ever seeing such splendour again (1980, 275–76).

References

Johnson, G.
1985 'Taking Fidelity Philosophically', in J. Graham (ed), *Difference in Translation*, Cornell University Press, Ithaca.

Jordon, A.C.
1940 *Ingqumbo Yeminyanya*, The Lovedale Press, Lovedale.
1980 *The Wrath of the Ancestors*, translated by the author with the help of Priscilla P. Jordan, The Lovedale Press, Lovedale. .

Kunene, D.
1981 Translation of *Chaka* by Thomas Mofolo, Heinemann, London.

Newmark, P.
1981 *Approaches to Translation*, Pergamon Press, Oxford.

Rose, M.G.
1981 'Introduction: Time and Space in the Translation Process', in M.G. Rose (ed), *Translation Spectrum*, State University of New York Press, Albany.

Ross, S.D.
1981 'Translation and Similarity', in M.G. Rose (ed), *Translation Spectrum*, State University of New York Press, Albany.

Activism and Criticism During the Black Arts Movement

Theodore R Hudson

From the late 1950s into the 1970s there evolved in United States' literature a phenomenon that we now identify as the Black Arts Movement, a sort of second Harlem Renaissance, if you will. A difference between the two, although they were alike in many important respects, is that the Black Arts Movement writers consciously strove to create new forms for what they considered to be new ideas, new attitudes, new tactics. As one writer put it, they sought to create a 'post-America form'.

With this explosion of new Afro-American writing arose the need for a re-examination of traditional criteria for literature, and there arose the need for critics to analyse and to assay and to assess this new writing. Larry Neal (1968, 20), a key theorist during the Black Arts Movement, declared, '...the Black Arts Movement proposes a radical reordering of the western cultural aesthetic. It proposes a separate symbolism, mythology, critique, and iconology.'

At the beginning of the 1960s there was, in contrast to that of a decade later, precious little criticism of Afro-American writing by Afro-American critics. Why was this so? Why had there been relatively few black, or (as the term was then) Negro, critics of Negro literature?

For one thing, before the 1960s Afro-American critics, for the most part, were academicians in predominantly black institutions of higher learning. In these generally understaffed and underbudgeted colleges and universities, they were so tied down by demanding teaching schedules and so tied down by administrative, clerical, and co-curricular chores that they simply had little time for the research, reflection, and writing that their counterparts in white institutions had.

For another thing, the Afro-American academicians received little encouragement to engage in consideration of Afro-American writing. Only traditional English and American literature, well established as canon, were considered worthy of their time and energy and talent. Sterling Brown, for instance, a pre-eminent Afro-American literary historian and critic, was adversely criticised by one of his colleagues as wasting time with that 'nigger' literature.

Third, there were practically no forums for Afro-American critics of Afro-American writing. Most criticism of it appeared in a few publications, most of these not primarily devoted to literature. Titles that come to mind include

Crisis, Opportunity, Negro Digest and *Journal of Negro History. Crisis* was the periodical of the politically and socially attuned National Association for the Advancement of Colored People. *Opportunity* was the official publication of the Urban League. *Negro Digest* was essentially a general purpose, popular publication. *The Journal of Negro History* was published by the history oriented Association for the Study of Negro Life and History. Of course, there were a few black newspapers that published occasional brief reviews. What about the major, white publications? Criticism of Afro-American writing, when it was published, in forums such as the New York *Times, Atlantic,* and *New Republic* was done by whites. In the rare instances when these established, powerful media did use Afro-American reviewers, they usually chose a 'name' black, usually not from among trained black critics and scholars, but from among better known black writers or leaders, for example a Langston Hughes.

In short, criticism of black writing was controlled by whites. What creative writer Ishmael Reed said recently about two current white critics of black writing is descriptive of that time too. Reed (1978, 33) said that white critics 'are really only moonlighting when they write critiques of Afro-American literature'. Indeed, the first book-length criticism of Afro-American writing in the evolving Black Arts Movement was by whites such as David Littlejohn, Edward Margolies, Abraham Chapman, Robert Bone—all perhaps well intentioned but relatively naive about the black experience in the United States.

Earlier I used the term 'precious little' to indicate the quality and quantity of criticism of Afro-American writing by Afro-Americans before the Black Arts Movement. I used the term advisedly, for although there was little, what there was was precious, of high quality. At least two generations of black critics, for example, preceded those of the Black Arts Movement. The work of the immediate forerunners—all academicians, incidentally Blyden Jackson, Therman O'Daniel, Saunders Redding, Sterling Brown, Nick Aaron Ford, Arthur P Davis, Hugh Gloster, and others—was first-rate and has stood the test of time. In the generation before them there were Afro-Americans who, in their varied writing on varied subjects in varied fields occasionally produced what might be classified as literary criticism. These earlier critics include prominently William DuBois, James Weldon Johnson and Alain Locke. None of these could be called primarily literary people. DuBois was a sociologist and thinker, Johnson was well known for his work as executive director of the National Association for the Advancement of Colored People, and Locke was a philosophy professor. All, however, were of great influence in the world of Afro-American letters. By the end of the 1960s these first-rate critics from the two preceding generations were followed by a generation of budding Black Arts Movement critics.

The chapter title, 'Activism and Criticism During the Black Arts Movement', indicates co-existence and interaction as well as cause-and-effect relationship between activism and criticism. Attempting to establish such causal factors between specific critics/criticism is risky business. It invites all sorts of non-sequiturs; all sorts of wide and wild inductive leaps; all sorts of tenuous links. This being so, it is well to think of activism as catalytic as well as causal, as co-existent as well as stimulative, as effect as well as cause. Thus, this Chapter proposes to be a summary statement of these various interactions.

As to definitions, I invite the readers to think of 'activism' in a broad sense of the term so that it encompasses not only overt, public, physical activism but also that it includes philosophical, aesthetic and intellectual activism. As to the term 'literary criticism', I invite the readers to think of it in a broad sense so that it encompasses interpretative and analytical criticism, explication, literary history, theoretical criticism and evaluative criticism.

These terms noted, let us now proceed as follows: first, we will note five facets, or types, of Afro-American activism operative in the United States during the 1960s and into the 1970s. Then we will, again in summary fashion, note the effects and concomitants of these types of activism in the criticism.

The first type of activism is so obvious that it does not require much exposition at all. This activism is the matrix of events, or happenings, that may be grouped under the labels of the Civil Rights Movement, the Black Power Movement, and the Black Arts Movement. A word about these labels: the Civil Rights Movement began with the social changes wrought during the decade or so, beginning in the mid-1950s, when Martin Luther King Jr, and his philosophy of passive resistance, moral suasion, non-violent protest, and redemptive love seized the imagination and set the tone and methods for social change for Afro-Americans. The second label, the Black Power Movement, came about, in part, because of younger Afro-Americans' impatience and disillusionment with King's philosophy and methods and because of their perception of white America's respect, not for King's moral imperatives but rather for power imperatives, that is, respect for force, for militancy, for aggression, for violence. As one Black Power activist said, the only thing that non-violent methods had proved was how violent white people could be. Black Power advocates asked, had not three little black girls been bombed to death in a Birmingham, Alabama church; had not two key leaders, John F Kennedy and Malcolm X, been struck down by assassins' bullets; had not white men sworn to uphold law and order turned fire hoses and police dogs on peaceful, non-violent petitioners; had not freedom riders been brutally attacked while officers of the law looked on? And so their philosophy was to meet force with force, to gain respect and rights through overt confrontation and aggression. The various urban uprisings, or riots: in Watts, California; in Newark, New Jersey; in Detroit, Michigan; and in other places and almost nationally at the time of the assassination of Martin Luther King Jr are marking points for this new era of Afro-American evolution speeding toward revolution. An integral part of this overall struggle for social justice, especially during the Black Power Movement, was the Black Arts Movement. One critic rightly declared the Black Arts Movement to be the cultural arm of the Black Power Movement. Thus, Afro-American critics were inescapably concerned with the content of Afro-American writing, whether it be social, political, economic, spiritual, or whatever.

In addition to generally public events that occurred during these movements, there were in them events of particular importance to the Afro-American literary world. Let me give a few examples: one phenomenon was a group of very young writers in New York City and their magazine, entitled *Umbra*, meaning 'darkest part of a shadow'. Many literary historians consider their publication, begun in 1963, as the beginning of the new Afro-American writing that flourished in the Black Arts Movement. Still another example is the Fisk University Writers Conference in 1967, a gathering of bold, irreverent, energetic young writers bent on sociopolitical and artistic revolution. Still another example is the international Festival of Negro Arts in Dakar, Senegal in 1966 that focused Afro-American artists' attention on commonalities among peoples of the African Diaspora. There were many more cultural innovations in the field of literature, including the Black Arts Repertory Theatre/School in Harlem, the somewhat later formed Organization of Black American Culture (OBAC) in Chicago, and BLKARTSOUTH writers in New Orleans. In various ways all of these movements and events and organisations helped create an enabling climate for and a need for Afro-American recorders, interpreters, spokespeople, and, germane to the present discussion, critics of Afro-American letters.

A second type of activism, an extremely important type, was the creation of forums for Afro-American writers and critics. Afro-American periodicals increased dramatically in number. Of almost incalculable significance was the magazine *Black World*, which under the editorship of Hoyt Fuller had evolved from the bland *Negro Digest*. The first issue, in 1961, contained a prophetically entitled essay by Arna Bontemps, this title being 'The New Black Renaissance'. Other publications that sprang up in the 1960s include—and notice these titles as indicators of the temper of the time—*Freedomways, Confrontation* (three issues), *Black Scholar, Liberator, Black America*, the aforementioned *Umbra*, and *Black Books Bulletin*, although its first distribution was not until 1970.

As we note the inception of certain of these periodicals, we can see direct links between community activism and literary criticism, for a number of these periodicals were created by what we might call street, or community, activists. Good examples are some publications that originated in the San Francisco area of California. Again, notice titles such as *Black Dialogue, Black Drama, Soul Book*, and *Black Panther*. A word about several of them: *Phase II; Journal of Black Arts Renaissance* came out of intellectual and cultural activist Sarah Webster Fabio's classes in Oakland, California, classes that included community activists who were to become known later. For example, one, Bobby Seale, was to become internationally known for his activities with the Black Panthers. *Black Dialogue*, another activist publication, was started by Art Sheridan, a student at San Francisco State

College. Although to be accurate it must be said that *Black Dialogue* began after the first bona fide student activists had left San Francisco State College. Another publication, *Black Drama*, came into existence through the efforts of community activist Marvin X and community and college activist Ed Bullins, who was later to be a leading Black Arts Movement dramatist. *Black Panther*, of course, was the organ of the Black Panther Party, the most intimidating organisation of the era. *Soul Book* was supported by Bobby Seale, Ernie Allen, Ken Freeman, Marvin X, and others who considered themselves revolutionaries of one sort or another. *The Journal of Black Poetry*, a sort of spin-off from *Black Dialogue*, indirectly grew out of ferment caused by community and black studies activists, although its editor, Joe Goncalves, probably would not consider himself a community activist. The important thing for us to remember in connection with these activist-generated publications is that they provided a forum for formal and informal criticism of Afro-American writing and set the tone for critics' philosophical bases for discussion of Afro-American writing.

Not only did Afro-American critics find a forum in new periodicals. Traditional scholarly journals such as *American Literature* and *PMLA* (Publications of Modern Language Association) began publishing occasional pieces by Afro-Americans about Afro-American writing. And, as one might expect, the few Afro-American controlled publications increased their attention to less traditional critical concerns. Let me underscore this assertion with some statistics provided by A Russell Brooks, a long-time member of the predominantly black College Language Association (CLA), which publishes the well respected *CLA Journal*. The period covered by Professor Brooks's statistics are the two succeeding decades 1957–67 and 1967–77. Brooks (1982, 7) reports:

> The number of articles on ethnic-related material increased from 63 in the first decade to 300 in the second; on non-ethnic-related subjects, there was a decrease from 155 to 112. Compared with 52 black writing on black subjects in the first period, there were 211 in the second. ...in the first decade for every one article on ethnic-related subjects, there were 2.4 on non-ethnic... For the second decade the ratio of ethnic to non-ethnic subjects was 2.6 to 1.

Such old and new publications as we have mentioned provided a forum for the work of most of the Afro-American critics who are of stature today, for instance, Darwin Turner, Addison Gayle, George Kent, and Eugenia Collier.

A third form of activism was the establishment of black presses. Black Power and Black Arts theorists, perceiving indifference and/or outright opposition to Afro-Americans' interests and ideas on the part of white presses, called for black-owned and black-controlled publishing companies. Those that were established as a result of this thinking were few, and these few were indeed modest in size. Yet they were of great importance to Afro-American letters.

I would say that the most important of these presses during the Black Arts Movement was Dudley Randall's Broadside Press, practically a one-person operation. Randall was quick to publish relatively unknown and obscure creative writers as somewhat established writers. Many of his authors he published in book-form for the first time. Sonia Sanchez, one of the leading Afro-American poets, is an example. Her first book-length work, *Homecoming*, was published by Randall when she was a relatively unknown young poet. As Broadside grew in strength and reputation, Randall published a few book-length works by Afro-American critics.

Another key publishing enterprise is Haki Madhubuti's (Don L Lee's) Third World Press, still in existence but not very active. Others that provided forums for both writers and literature commentators include Black Poetry Press, Black Dialogue Press, Drum and Spear Press. And, though not a publisher in the usual sense of the word, well worthy of inclusion is Julian Richardson, the San Francisco printer off whose presses rolled works by the so-called mother of the Black Studies Movement, Sarah Webster Fabio; off whose presses rolled various Black Panther publications; off whose presses rolled the periodicals *Black Dialogue, Journal of Black Poetry,* and *Soul Book.*

Few of these publishing companies that I have named printed much criticism during the 1960s, but they are significant in the world of criticism in that they contributed new material for criticism and in that they created a climate for black writing and publishing that was encouraging to black critics and would-be critics.

A fourth form of activism was the Black Studies Movement, a movement that came about mainly because of Afro-American students' insistence that they be provided formal academic studies in their history and culture. As noted earlier, before the Black Arts Movement, the black academic critics— few in number—at both predominantly black and predominantly white institutions taught and did their research and writing in white, or traditional, mainly Western literary fields. The Black Studies Movement created a situation in which previously repressed and closeted and potential black academic critics and scholars could write. Moreover, the Black Studies Movement created more positions for black critics and scholars on campuses of white institutions where they found themselves freed from the budget-imposed, tradition-imposed and attitude-imposed restrictions on time and facilities for writing. Arna Bontemps, Richard Barksdale, Addison Gayle, Houston Baker, Charles Davis, and the like—all respected for their criticism of Afro-American writing and all of whom teach or taught at major, predominantly white colleges and institutions—found more time for and more facilities for scholarly productivity and literary criticism than their counterparts at black institutions found. This is not to say that critics and scholars on black campuses did not have increased opportunities as a result of the Black Studies Movement. I am referring to degree. Certainly with the advent of black studies, critics and scholars on black campuses found more than ever before more release time, better physical facilities, more financial support in the form of grants and awards, and most important, more support and encouragement, official and unofficial, from their colleagues and administrators than they and their predecessors had found.

And now to the last type of activism that I will touch upon— intellectual activism. With the plethora of new Afro-American writing came the need for new criticism. The efforts of white critics of black writing were considered, for the most part, uninformed, myopic, non-empathetic, shallow or biased. White critics such as Robert Bone, David Littlejohn, Edward Margolies were looked upon with benign suspicion or, at the extreme, with contempt. Consider, for instance, a statement by a relatively young black critic, Sherley Anne Williams. She begins by acknowledging that 'White critics have every right to comment upon any literature'. But then Williams (1972, 234) goes on to say:

> with only the rarest exceptions, white critics have proved time and again that their perceptions are neither deep enough or precise enough to give us the insights we need into our literature and our experience.

Consider also a statement by Hoyt Fuller (1967, 9), at that time editor of the magazine *Black World*:

> The white world is simply not qualified or prepared to evaluate Black writing, and consequently the task of setting up standards which will realistically deal with Black writers must fall to the Black community where it belongs.

Now, having heard these examples of anti-white assertions regarding critics of black literature, let us now hear pro-black assertions, the first of these by Hoyt Fuller (1968, 9), who hoped for:

> the emergence of new black critics who will be able to articulate and expound the new aesthetic and eventually set in motion the long overdue assault against the restrictive assumptions of the white critics.

Hear, too, the words of Don L Lee (1970, 137), later to be known as Haki Madhubuti:

> [the] critic is first and foremost a blackman, a redman, yellowman or whiteman who writes. And as a critic, he must stem from the roots that produced him.

Regardless of the blackness or whiteness of the critics, the new Afro-American writing called for specialised attention. The words of Larry Neal (1968, 20) previously quoted bear repeating for their summary value:

> the Black Arts Movement proposes a radical reordering of the western cultural aesthetic. It proposes a separate symbolism, mythology, critique, and iconology.

The calls for a new critique and for new critics were answered.

Implicit in such calls by intellectual activists for black critics was the need for these critics to investigate questions about the nature and function of art, specifically in regard to the art of writing, and more specifically in regard to the function, nature, and aesthetics of black literature.

So much for the five forms of activism that directly and indirectly contributed to the birth of a generation of new Afro-American critics and criticism and that contributed to renewed attention to theories about literature.

The next question is, in terms of achievements and shortcomings, what elements or characteristics of literature resulted? I am now shifting a bit from essentially reportorial, or expository discussion to what may lean toward perceptual, judgemental discussion.

First, let me comment on the negative characteristics. I think that the activism of the times fostered too much of what I call hagiographic, or praise, criticism. Black Power activists—and this is of crucial importance in regard to those who controlled periodicals—were saying that Afro-Americans are engaged in a revolution, a war—an ideological and economic and political and perhaps imminent physical war. Roberta Sykes's quotation of Pablo Neruda in her keynote speech to the Conference on Black Literatures (see Appendix), 'Come and see the blood in the streets!' may be applied to militants who saw ivory tower writers among black critics. And in time of war, a participant, in this instance a critic, does not unfavourably criticise loyal and brave soldiers, in this instance loyal and brave word soldiers. As critic Jerry Ward (1980, 21) looks back and says:

> In the 1960s, the ideological climate was such that critics who would be heard had to describe the function of literature according to the rhythms of social struggle.

Because they were caught up in the revolutionary zeal of the times, too few critics, it seems to me, in that time of jingoistic criticism, spoke out, rightly or wrongly, in the manner of Sherley Anne Williams and Stanley Crouch. Williams observed (1972, 240):

> Every piece of writing with choppy non-sentences, perverted word order and four letter words set in stanzaic form on a piece of paper is not a poem, although its revolutionary zeal may be patent.

Crouch offered the opinion that (1968, 28):

> One of the major problems in Black writing is that most of the people who pass themselves off as writers either cannot write, are capitalizing on something that has moved from true feeling to a name-calling fad masked as 'Revolutionary Black nationalism', or, they have no respect for the craft.

Unfortunately, some activists considered any critic who analysed form, or technique, as being a proponent of art-for-art's-sake, that is, a proponent of white art, or Euro-American art, as opposed to black art. What they wanted was, to use the term by Don L Lee, art-for-people's-sake. The point is that, in my view, critics were overlooking or excusing writing that was of such inferior quality that it would do little to help, and perhaps ultimately could negatively affect the struggle in which Afro-Americans were engaged.

A corollary of what I call hagiographic criticism, a sin of omission, is that there was relatively too little inductive, descriptive, objective analysis and research of Afro-American writing. There were too few Steve Hendersons.

Henderson, in preparing his book *Understanding the New Black Poetry*, subtitled *Black Speech and Black Music as Poetic References*, very carefully examined inductively what existed and on the basis of that careful examination came to grips with what, if anything, is essentially black about black poetry.

Another corollary of this hagiographic criticism is prescriptive criticism, a sin of commission. Consider that many blacks in the literary world subscribed to the theory that black art 'must expose the enemy, praise the people, and support the revolution'. Too often critics, it seems to me, presumed to tell creative writers what and how they should create. Often they reasoned deductively, but began with shaky or theoretical major premises. These prescriptionists published didactic pieces in which they set down the 'role of' or a 'blueprint for' or the 'criteria for' or the 'function of' Afro-American creative artists. It seems to me that the word creative in the term creative writer was neither fully understood nor fully respected by these prescriptionists. Too few critics pushed an idea that creative writer Ntozake Shange pointed out later in another context, this idea being that each creative writer, as is the case with the creative black musician, must have his or her own voice. I must add at this point that I am again referring to degree, not absolutism.

Now for positive results of Black Arts Movement activism and criticism. I will note what I consider the most outstanding ones, for there were and are many, many more than the just-mentioned negative results.

Earlier in the Chapter I stated that intellectual activists' calls for a new critique forced Afro-American critics to deal with important questions and issues about the nature and function of art. This, of course, is an important positive result.

Another positive outcome is obvious to us in retrospect: a generation of excellent black critics, popularist critics included, came into being to develop and to continue the excellent work of the too few forerunner critics. Listen to a partial line-up of the present generation of critics: Amiri Baraka, earlier known as LeRoi Jones, Addison Gayle, Richard Long, the recently deceased Larry Neal, Claudia Tate, Robert O'Meally, Trudier Harris, Thadious Davis, and Ron Baxter Miller—the list goes on and on.

A third positive factor is that the generation of black critics spawned in the 1960s, generally speaking, provided fairer, more perceptive, more empathetic, and more penetrating criticism of Afro-American writing than did the white critics of Afro-American writing who were providing much of the visible criticism at the beginning of the Black Arts Movement. Happily, this type of Afro-American criticism has not diminished since the Black Arts Movement. It continues strongly today.

A fourth positive result is the unprecedented legacy of critical articles, periodicals and books. There are now countless articles. There are now scores of bibliographies. I earlier mentioned just a few of the periodicals. As to books, in the 1960s we had the publication of LeRoi Jones's *Home*, Harold Cruse's

The Crisis of the Negro Intellectual, Addison Gayle's *Black Expression*, Mercer Cook and Stephen Henderson's *The Militant Black Writer in Africa and the United States*, Don L Lee's *Dynamite Black Voices*, and others. Shortly thereafter, in the very early 1970s there were published, having been started or researched in the 1960s, Sherley Anne Williams's *Give Birth to Blackness*, Donald Gibson's *Five Black Writers*, Stephen Henderson's *Understanding the New Black Poetry*, George Kent's *Blackness and the Adventure of Western Culture*, and Addison Gayle's *Black Expression: A Gathering of Essays by and about Black Americans in the Creative Arts*. All of these books and more are worthy of the most serious study by the most serious students and scholars in the field of literature.

Finally, Afro-American critics during the Black Arts Movement introduced into the broad field of scholarly discourse about literature, the crucial theory of a Black Aesthetic. (Anyone interested in this theory would do well to begin with Addison Gayle's *The Black Aesthetic*.) Faced with pronouncements such as 'The purpose of black literature is to make revolution irresistible', they raised and forced discussion on the proper questions. Is there, indeed, a Black Aesthetic? What distinguishes a piece of literature as black? Is it possible or even desirable to create a new, that is, uniquely black literature within the rubric of Western literature? What are the necessary qualifications for a critic of black literature? Can existing genre criteria be applied to black literature? Is the Black Aesthetic prescriptive or descriptive in nature? Which should it be? To what extent, if any, is ideological 'correctness' a criterion for black literature? Who should be the target readership for black literature? Is the term 'polemical literature' a self-contradiction? What makes a writer black? Are fair parallels to the Black Arts Movement found in, say, the Celtic revival? What is universality as it applies to literature?

It is my contention that in grappling with these questions, Black Arts Movement critics grappled with the overriding question about all writing: What, in fact, is artistic literature?

References

Brooks, R.
1982 'The *CLA Journal* as a Mirror of Changing Ethnic and Academic Perspectives'. Paper presented at the College Language Association annual convention, Charlotte, North Carolina, 23 April 1983.

Crouch, S.
1968 'Toward a Purer Black Poetry Aesthetic', *Journal of Black Poetry*, Fall, 28–33.

Cruse, H.
1984 *The Crisis of the Negro Intellectual*, Morrow, New York (reprint).

Fuller, H.
1967 'Black Writing Is Socio-Creative Art', *Liberator*, April, 7–10.
1968 'Towards a Black Aesthetic', *The Critic*, April–May, 7–9.

Gayle, A.
1969 *Black Expression*, Weybright and Talley, New York.
1971 *Black Aesthetic*, Doubleday, Garden City, New York.

Gibson, D.
1970 *Five Black Writers*, New York University Press, New York.

Henderson, S.
1973 *Understanding the New Black Poetry*, Morrow, New York.

Henderson, S. and Cook, M.
1969 *Militant Black Writer in Africa and the United States*, University of Wisconsin Press, Madison.

Jones, L.
1966 *Home*, Morrow, New York.

Kent, G.
1972 *Blackness and the Adventure of the Western World*, Third World Press, Chicago.

Lee, D.
1970 *Dynamite Voices*, Broadside Press, Detroit.

Neal, L.
1968 'The Black Arts Movement', *The Drama Review*, 4, 20–25.

Reed, I.
1978 'A Conversation with John Domini', *American Poetry Review*, January–February, 32–34.

Ward, J.
1980 'The Black Critic as Reader', *Black American Literature Forum*, 1, 20–24.

Williams, S.
1972 *Give Birth to Blackness*, Dial, New York.

Ed Bullins: Black Theatre as Ritual

Arlene A Elder

In 1971, the African-American playwright, Ed Bullins (1973, 12) said of himself, 'To make an open secret more public: in the area of playwrighting, Ed Bullins, at this moment in time, is almost without peer in America—black, white, or imported'. Fortunately, time has supported this boast. In a recent assessment, critic Genevieve Fabre (1983, 168) concludes, 'Next to LeRoi Jones, Ed Bullins is probably the most important black dramatist of the last twenty years'.

Bullins's continuing success rests for some in his political stance, expressive, largely but not entirely, of the Black Power interpretation of a racist American society. For many others, it rests with his sensitivity to the artistic imperatives of Black Aesthetic theory, that is, to the return to traditional, African oral performance and African-American folk roots. These two impulses are not, of course, mutually exclusive; they are, however, difficult to reconcile successfully in a single artistic work. Such reconciliation requires not only talent but, also, a clear understanding of the purposes of one's art and of the playwright's role *vis a vis* his audience.

This dilemma of the contemporary black artist is one not lost on literary critics. Peter Bruck (1979, 52), for example, in an article entitled, 'Ed Bullins: The Quest and Failure of an Ethnic Community Theatre', quotes the following paradoxical statements by Bullins:

> I hope that all of us will...produce create, that is, for we are creators, revolution. And that, I think, is the true role of the revolutionary artist. Black Art is to express what is best in us and for us Black People. Black Theater is...a people's theater, dedicated to the continuing survival of Black people.

'How does one', Bruck asks (1979, 52), 'aesthetically speaking, reconcile the hope for revolution with the wish for survival? In other words, how are the two aspirations to be combined in theater politics?'

Bruck resolves the paradox satisfactorily for himself by placing Bullins's work within the historical context of Alain Locke's (1969, 125) distinction during the 1920s between 'the drama of discussion and social analysis and the drama of expression of folk life' and seeing Bullins combining these two dichotomies. Expressing both a Marxist and a Black Aesthetic perspective, Bruck says Bullins represents (1979, 53):

a new stage in the evolution of black drama. As his plays are beset with urban *lumpen* blacks and their sub-cultural lifestyle of hustling, he transcends both the realm of mere social analysis and of a mere portrayal of folk life by seeking to fuse these realms in the minute depiction of various facets of black existence.

Although the Marxist analysis is obviously useful (and, indeed a feminist perspective is called for as well), this fusion in Bullins's plays can best be understood, by examining the work through the Black Aesthetic as examples of contemporary rituals and by recognising the playwright's conscious desire to reawaken the power of this ancient form in his audience. Bullins (1979, 109), himself, has suggested this approach to his work. 'Perhaps', he says, 'the black artist should think in the ancient tribal patterns, in the terms of his people as tribal units, and he being the shaman, sorcerer, medicine man or witch doctor.' Acutely aware of the possible polarities of contemporary black theatre, Bullins (1979, 109) explains, 'I was a conscious artist before I was a conscious artist revolutionary, which has been my salvation and disguise'.

Plays such as 'The Corner', 'In the Wine Time', and 'In New England Winter', are three works intended as part of his ongoing Twentieth Century Cycle and concern the fortunes and relationships of Cliff Dawson and his half-brother, Steve Benson. In these plays, Bullins clearly demonstrates this conscious return to the elements of traditional African oral performance and African-American folk roots. These plays, among others, reveal his ability to couch revolutionary interpretations of the black American experience in ritual form, drawing on the traditions of black oratory, narrative, street talk, mythology, and, especially, music.

When one reads Black Aesthetic theory, it soon becomes clear that there is no consensus of opinion as to what contemporary black rituals are, precisely, and how the literate playwright should utilise this oral and aural form. The loosest definition is that of critic Shelby Steele (1980, 30), who views 'the ritualistic aspect' of the New Black Theatre as one of its 'most salient characteristics' separating it 'from mainstream American drama'. By 'ritualistic', Steele means (1980, 30):

> the strong presence of *symbols, characterizations, themes* and *language styles* which are frequently repeated from play to play and over a period of time with the result that easily recognized patterns are established which have the function of reaffirming the values and particular commitment of the audience for whom the plays are written. The term *ritual* is used here in the modern sense which is looser than the traditional religious view of ritual as a rigidly prescribed unvarying pattern of spiritual observance.

It is, however, toward 'spiritual observance' that the director, Robert Macbeth, with whom Bullins had a very close association during their years together at The New Lafayette Theatre, wishes to move. Macbeth, whom Bullins credits along with Imamu Baraka as having had a profound influence upon him, has spoken very persuasively about the function of ritual in contemporary black theatre. His goal for performances at The New Lafayette suggests drama that is much more religiously oriented than what Steele has in mind. He explains (Marvin X 1970, 24):

> we would like to return to...those rituals that our people did in ancient times, rituals that taught the young men the essence of courage and manhood. Rituals that showed the young women their place in the history of their people. These are plain, old, ordinary, educational ones. Then there are the more mystic ones, the more spiritual ones, and those are the ones that call upon the ancient Black gods, and call upon the spirits of the fathers, and the spirit of the ancestors to be of importance in the present as we continue.... I think we're preparing our people, The New Lafayette audience, for that time into participating in a ritual in which the spells are cast, in which new vibrations are created that never existed before.

The traditional African concept of art's functional significance is also important to Macbeth (1972, 18):

> Our people's rituals are never just for show, they're always for purpose, they're always for something...something for the purpose of entertainment is not part of our people's reality in that sense. When they get together, it's not for entertainment, it's for unity, for being together, for having a time together.

Unlike Steele, Macbeth is clearly not using the term, 'ritual', in a modern sense, but in ancient terms that he is confident will have spiritual and, consequently, political consequences for the future. Macbeth's 1968 'A Black Ritual' is the type of performance he hoped would soon characterise much of black theatre. Clearly, a conventional playwright would have to revolutionise his artistic choices, even his understanding of himself as an artist and transform even the performance oriented techniques of conventional black drama to create such a theatrical experience as Macbeth's 'A Black Ritual'.

Ed Bullins's plays reveal a movement toward such development, and statements by him and Macbeth place his understanding of ritual somewhere between the previous loose version by Steele and the more rigorous one of Macbeth.

Bullins's list of the 'obvious elements' that should constitute black plays shows his appreciation of the spiritual or mystical dimension of traditional performance. He calls for (1972, 9):

> dance, as in Black life style and patterns; Black religion in its numerous forms...gospel, negro spiritualism to African spirit, sun, moon, stars and ancestor worship; Black astrology, numerology and symbolism; Black mysticism, magic and mythscience; also history, fable and legend, vodun ritual ceremony, Afro-American nigger street styles, and, of course, Black music.

However, Bullins still writes plays, recognisable as such by audiences formally trained in Aristotelean dramatic principles as well as those schooled in African orature and black street styles of performance. His works, then, provide the largest number of examples of that middle ground in black drama that Robert Macbeth designates 'play form rituals' (Marvin X 1970, 18). The spiritual effect of these plays depends as much upon the way they are staged as upon the texts, hence upon the director almost as much as the playwright. Director Macbeth judges his production of 'In the Wine Time' and other plays at The New Lafayette Theatre as revealing the company's 'ritual point of view' (Marvin X 1970, 18):

> We always try to approach (the play) from the point of view of a service, a ritual of some kind, and for that reason, because we approach them that way, our plays are a little bit different in a lot of things, the timing, the way the thing gets done, the way it's staged, how it's staged, why it's staged that way.

Speaking specifically of 'In the Wine Time', he is pleased with his staging, because it (Marvin X 1970, 18):

> includes the people in there so they understand this thing is between us, among us all. ...the thing that we begin to do immediately includes all the people who come. So all of these things are orientated around, 'Welcome, sit down, Brother, we're gonna hold hands and sing...'.

This statement was made in 1970. A year later, however, Macbeth (Neal 1971, 21) admits to the possibly insurmountable difficulties in the Western dramatic form, which he calls, 'really ragged' and 'very hard'; 'it doesn't serve our purposes', he realises. Of special concern is the audience's separation from the action, not just physically but, also in terms of roles and responsibilities, hence, spiritual fulfilment. 'I did want you to talk back during the play', he explains to an audience member of 'In the Wine Time'. 'You were supposed to get into it. But the form is limited. It doesn't really work. The Western white form is a drawing room form. They sit around and they jive. They sit there and talk to each other. Nothing really happens.' Therefore, he desires the movement to a more traditional ritual form mentioned earlier, where audience members can participate, in playwright and theorist, Paul Carter Harrison's (1972, 8) term, as 'spectator performers'.

Whatever the limitations of the 'play-form ritual', Ed Bullins (1972, 14) views theatre in the black community as 'a sanctuary for recreation of the Black spirit and African identity'. Bullins has been at work for some time on a series of twenty plays he envisions as the Twentieth Century Cycle, focusing primarily on the lives of one family and different acquaintances. The following is a commentary on three of these plays, 'The Corner', 'In the Wine Time', and 'In New England Winter', all of which present stages in the life of Cliff Dawson and his half-brother, Steve, and, specifically, examines them as 'play-form rituals'.

Briefly, the narrative of the three interlocking plays is as follows: 'The Corner', the shortest of the three, presents the conflicts over wine, women, and self-image of four, young, urban blacks, one of whom is Cliff Dawson, who by the end of the play has stunned his friends by deciding to quit wasting his money, his time, and life, drinking every night under the street lamp on the corner or on the back seat of a broken-down car with Stella. The reason for this change is, most immediately, his acceptance of responsibility as the father of his other girlfriend Lou's unborn child and, of more long-range significance, his desire for a more meaningful future than that promised by hanging out on the corner.

'In the Wine Time', picks up a little later in Cliff's life with Lou, when she is about three months pregnant. We learn that Cliff had, at one time, been in the Navy and is now going to night school. Bullins is still interested in evoking the atmosphere of his characters' poor, urban neighbourhood, but the most important action in the play consists of conflicts between Lou and Cliff about how to raise her nephew, Ray. The climax occurs when Ray stabs another youth, and to save him, Cliff takes the blame.

'In New England Winter' is set several years later, after Cliff has gotten out of prison and has lost Lou, and centres on Cliff's half-brother, Steve, mentioned in 'The Corner' as having an unspecified disagreement with one of the other wine drinkers, Bummie. Here, the conflict takes the form not only of sibling rivalry between Cliff and Steve, but of two opposed lifestyles, that can be characterised simply as Western and non-Western. In the course of the play, it is revealed that Cliff has known for a long time that Lou's second child was by Steve. Nevertheless, when Steve kills Bummie, a cohort now in a robbery they have planned, Cliff once again devises a scheme to help save the younger brother.

As this synopsis indicates, these plays follow the traditional Western form of presenting a developing story. Moreover, they create individual characters who speak and interact in theatrically expected ways, and they are played out in a recognisable historical setting and time period—the late 1950s. When we analyse them as orature, however, not as literature, that is, when we examine their performance features, not just their lines of dialogue on a printed page, Bullins's ritualistic intent becomes clear.

First, despite my chronological presentation of their action, neither the plot of 'In the Wine Time' nor of 'In New England Winter' is actually linear. The first play opens with a dream-like reverie of Ray's about a Girl symbolic of all youth, innocence, and promise of love that cannot exist in his depressing, limiting street environment. She is the mother/lover who calls him her 'little boy' and invites him 'out in the world'. Her departure from the neighbourhood signals the end of his youth. In Act Two, the Girl, who is the romantic opposite of all the real girls he knows, reappears in a tableau as Ray talks to Cliff about her. Her reappearance signals a symbolic dance by the other characters, interrupting the realistic, chronological sequence of action and suggesting that symbolic action, psychological movement, is of the greatest importance in what, at first, appears to be a naturalistic play. 'I do not write realistic plays, no matter the style I choose' Bullins (1979, 109) has said.

'In New England Winter' bears him out. This 'play-form ritual' consists of seven titled sequences that are not at all sequential. Like 'In the Wine

Time', it, too, opens with a reverie, both of which have been published separately as pieces of fiction. Again, as in the other play, the content of this prologue is a love relationship, this time the aborted relationship between Steve and the mad Liz, during a winter in New England. It also presents, however, the carrying out of the robbery that is still being rehearsed and prepared for in the subsequent scenes of the play.

Section One pulls us into the present to the rehearsing of the robbery and to hear about what happened between Cliff and Lou while he was in prison. Sections Two and Three return us to Steve in New England with Liz. Section Four jumps to the present to further develop the conflict between the two brothers. Sections Five and Six detail Steve's break up with Liz in the past, and Section Seven gives us Steve's murder of Bummie in the present. Bullins's juxtaposition of non-sequential time periods, then, definitely distinguishes his works from those of the traditional Western 'well-made play' with its linear time requirements and demonstrates his allegiance to a symbolic, mythic, or psychological reality rather than to social realism or naturalism.

It is Bullins's allegiance to the African concept of the unity of the arts, however, and his development of representative black characters that convincingly demonstrates his commitment to revolutionary drama based on ancient forms. 'I believe my characters sometimes have multiple identities, as parts of a whole, as ever-changing, interchangeable universe (sic), as the points in a vision which expands—dreamlike', he says (1979, 109).

There is a dream-like quality to the three plays under discussion, much of it contributed to, of course, by the non-linear narrative technique, but also by the reappearance, as if recalled from some dream or previous life, of characters repeated from play to play. Cliff Dawson, for example, develops from the dissatisfied, aimless street kid of 'The Corner' to a father-figure for Ray in 'In the Wine Time', to one, in Bullins's terms, 'more resigned to the reality of his identity' in 'In New England Winter'. Cliff's metamorphosis as an individual is hopeful, because Bullins characterises it as a rejection of the dehumanising Western values still espoused by his younger brother, Steve.

Steve, whose relationship with Cliff's wife, Lou, has been forgiven, is the plotter of the robbery being planned in the play. He is associated throughout the work with cold, snow, winter, even winter's 'Silen(ce) like death must be' (1969a, 137). As Cliff realises, Steve resents him for being the elder and believes he had a closer relationship with their mother than he had. Steve continually compares himself favourably with Cliff, criticising his treatment of Lou and of women in general and, especially, what he perceives as his lack of seriousness.

While the spectator would expect the brothers to clash over Lou, then, their actual conflict is about their mother, a jealousy that remains unresolved, and, even more significantly, about lifestyles. Steve is anxious, methodical, future oriented; Cliff lives for the day, if not the moment, and expresses his feelings, his love for Steve, for instance, without fear. Steve seems machine-like to Cliff (1969a, 160):

> I'm not just talkin' about how you plan jobs, Steve. It's how you live...that's the part you can keep. Your bein' on time or you'll have a heart attack. Your keepin' to the schedules you make...whether it's takin' some bull-shit night course, gettin' your hair cut a certain time ah month...or waitin' for years to go see the woman you love.

When he rejects Cliff's expression of love for him, Steve explains (1969a, 162):

> No, I can't feel...don't want to if I could. That's for you, big boss. Me...I don't have feelings, emotions, sympathy, tenderness, compassion...none of it...I don't need it...it slows you up. I wouldn't have any of that sickness in me if I didn't have to deal with people like you.

Yet if Steve cannot act out of love, he can out of hate. He kills Bummie in a fit of passion, and it is Cliff, ironically, who must assume leadership and plan how to save him.

Bullins's characterisation seems intended to offer his audience two opposing lifestyles and to show his preference for love and involvement in life over detached self-interest. Criticised frequently for the depressing, criminal lifestyles of his characters, their 'offensive' language, and the violence in his plays, Bullins's (1972, 16) first reply is one establishing the authenticity of his portrayal: 'I learned how to survive. I'm a street nigger.' A later response, however, indicates the cathartic, spiritual intent of his work. He explains that he wishes to make 'the members of (the) community see themselves in all their terrible ugliness in hope that from this profound glimpse they will be cleansed' (Smitherman 1974, 5–6).

As Paul Carter Harrison has pointed out, this catharsis requires the natural, active involvement of the audience, a dynamic best achieved through the arts of music and dance. 'Music is one of the most effective modes of unifying the black community', Harrison observes (1972, 56), 'it unveils an emotional potency and spiritual force that is collectively shared. Black music articulates the cross-fertilization of African sensibility and the American experience...'. Critics have noted not only the actual presence of music in most of Bullins's plays but, also, the essentially musical quality of their structure. Speaking of the 1968 'Goin' a Buffalo', Fabre (1983, 175) cautions, for instance:

> One must listen to Bullins' plays as one listens to music and be drawn into the movement of broken rhythms, dramatic breaks, repeats, and lyrical crescendos. The play unfolds like a musical score; each sequence has its own key and modality, each character a voice and register.

From within Cliff and Lou's house in 'In the Wine Time', black music of the period—called rhythm 'n blues by disc jockeys at that time—is heard not too loudly, and continues throughout the play, interrupted only seldom by amusing, jive-talking commercials. Some of the recording stars of this season are King Pleasure Johnnie Otis, Fats Domino, Little Esther, Ray Charles and 'the Queen' Miss Dinah Washington. 'When MISS MINNY GARRISON raises her window, gospel music can be heard' (1969b, 105–06). The mood of the later play, 'In New England Winter', is maintained by 'Modern jazz of the late fifties and early sixties, maybe Miles Davis or Cannonball or Nate Adderly' (1969a, 132). At Liz's place, 'Joe Williams sings "Goin to Chicago" over the drug store radio and Count Basie plays throughout the remainder of the scene' (1969a, 148). This music is not incidental but both reflective of the concerns and feelings of the characters and strategic in drawing the audience into the action, hence, in fulfilling the ritualistic intent of the plays.

As Askia Muhammed Toure (1968, 12) comments in *Black Theatre*, 'the Black musician became and remains the major philosopher, priest, myth-maker and cultural hero of the Black nation. ...Black music is the core of our National Culture.' Bullins's reliance upon this mode clearly indicates his understanding of the dramatic, political, and spiritual function of African orature. While LeRoi Jones's 'Slave Ship' is often pointed to as the best example of black ritual drama, Ed Bullins's 'play-form rituals' constitute the largest body of works combining aspects of the Western tradition with the revitalising features of the Black Aesthetic.

References

Bruck, P.
1979 'Ed Bullins: The Quest and Failure of an Ethnic Community Theatre', *Black American Literature Forum*, **13**, 50–54.

Bullins, E.
1969a 'In New England Winter', *New Plays from the Black Theatre*, Bantam, New York.
1969b 'In the Wine Time', *Five Plays*, Bobbs-Merrill, Indianapolis.
1972 'The Corner', *The Theme Is Blackness*, William Morrow, New York.
1979 'Who He is Now: Ed Bullins Replies', *Black American Literature Forum*, **13**, 109–10.

Fabre, G.
1983 *Drumbeats, Masks, and Metaphor*, Harvard University Press, Cambridge, Massachusetts.

Harrison, P.
1972 *The Drama of Nommo*, Grove Press, New York.

Locke, A.
1969 *Black Expression*, Weybright and Talley, New York.

Macbeth, R.
1972 'Macbeth Speaks', *Black Theatre*, **6**, 18–20.

Marvin X
1970 'The Black Ritual Theatre: An Interview with Robert Macbeth', *Black Theatre*,
   3, 18–25.

Neal, L.
1971 'Toward a Relevant Black Theatre', *Black Theatre*, **4**, 20–26.

Smitherman, G.
1974 'Ed Bullins/Stage One: Everybody Wants to Know Why I Sing the Blues', *Black
   World*, 23 April, 5–10.

Steele, S.
1980 'Notes on Ritual in the New Black Theater', in E. Hill (ed), *The Theater of Black
   Americans*, Prentice-Hall, Englewood Cliffs.

Toure, A.
1968 'The Crisis in Black Culture', *Black Theatre*, **1**, 10–15.

Appendix
Keynote Address to the
Conference on Black Literatures

Roberta B Sykes

I'm honoured to have been asked to address such an auspicious gathering—even though by default. I've no doubt that Kevin Gilbert, who was originally to make this address this morning, regrets very much his inability to attend.

Over the next three days we'll all get to know each other better, and despite the fact that we have amongst us many distinguished visitors from the other side of the world, I'm sure we'll find we have a great deal in common.

Literature, as a subject, is divided into three parts—the writers, the process and the product. Writers, I feel, 'agonise' over their thoughts, they put their thoughts down on pieces of paper—which stay pieces of paper until someone reads them and analyses them for meaning—at which point they 'become' literature. Before that it's just scribbly bits on paper, writing. But everything that's written is not 'literature'. My grocery shopping list, no matter who reads it, and despite the fact that I have to agonise over it, never becomes literature.

I'm personally not as interested in literature, the pieces of paper, as I am writing—so my talk this morning is addressed to 'writers' more so than it is about literature—because without the writers there is no literature.

The subject of writing reminds me of an article I read years ago which likened the stages of writing to the stages of prostitution. This article said writers, like prostitutes, first do it in desperation, later because they like it, and finally they do it for money! This is a very interesting comparison which I've reflected on many times over the years. It may even be true, and if so it says a great deal about the difference in life expectancy between blacks and whites globally. I haven't yet met a black who has lived long enough to reach the luxurious position of being able to write solely for the money!

Indeed, it also says much about our political relationship with the powers that be. In Australia in 1987, we celebrate our nineteenth year of citizenship—and with that, our theoretic access to the corridors of power. As writers who are part of our desperate and struggling communities, we are still, as community citizens, held fast in the state of desperation.

I feel, and perhaps you will agree with me, that we have not, as a group, even reached the second stage where we might write because we like it. I am reminded of the words of a Chilean poet, Pablo Neruda, who, in a poem entitled 'Explico Algunas Cosas' meaning 'I am Explaining a Few Things', wrote:

> And you will ask: Why doesn't his poetry speak of dreams and leaves and
> the great volcanos of his native land?
> Come and see the blood in the streets.
> Come and see the blood in the streets.
> Come and see the blood in the streets!...

Well, we too do not write of the dreams or leaves or the magnificent features of our native land. Come and see the blood in our gaols! Come and see the blood of our dead infants in our corrugated iron shacks! Behold our wounds, and our tears!

I suggest that black writers are the public sounds of our community weeping.

Perhaps I hear murmurs of dissent. Are there some amongst us who do search their minds just for a 'topic'? Do we not all look only for vehicles—vehicles to convey our message? Whether through poetry, reviews, plays, books, or academic treatises—it seems to me we have in common 'the struggle' and that we write as an act of desperation! It's great that we are, at last, able to host a conference of this nature.

Let me change the subject now because I'd like to share with you some thoughts I have about our global situation, and about how we, as black writers, fit into this rapidly changing scenario. I do wish we had had more time to prepare ourselves, because events are hurtling upon us so fast, and it's going to be difficult for us to stay on top of our situation. Difficult, but not impossible.

The world is getting smaller. Everything happening anywhere impacts on us. This is demonstrated most prominently in our economy, where our imbalance of trade internationally now affects the jobs and livelihoods of many Australians. It affects the level of our social services—which is constantly being trimmed that the already poor can save our national economy! I don't have to tell you how many of those poor are black.

Now, if our American guests will excuse me, I have to say that my observations of Americans, and indeed even black Americans, is that they are parochial. After being in exile in America for three years, I can understand why—but I can't condone it. All the evening television news programmes carry approximately four minutes of 'foreign news', all of which are prefaced by 'Mr Reagan said today...'. Anything that Mr Reagan didn't comment on obviously didn't happen. The print media is almost as bad.

The virtual monopoly of the packaging and sale of international news to print and electronic media by UPI and Reuters is a scandal. News from non-white countries is meagre, and when available is sensationalist. African countries suffer not only by how they are projected by this system, but also because they are unable to get any news about any other black peoples. Consequently, a very large portion of the world population, that is the entire black population, is not served by the existing news service. Not only does this inhibit the ability of black writers to make a living, but more importantly it maintains our isolation from each other.

We have to understand how dangerous we are as writers. Notice, for example, that the first thing to go in a state of emergency in South Africa is the freedom of the press. Indeed, for most of the white people in South Africa, only those involved in the press are really aware of the critical nature of events there, and then mainly because their own lives have been affected by it. For the blacks, however, things are going on as 'normal' because normal for them has always been a state of desperation, and they have never been in the position of either projecting or controlling their own image. Their place in the media is peripheral.

We have now a situation where white South Africans are fleeing that country and coming here. These are not liberals moving because they dislike apartheid—or they would have left years ago. These new boat people (so called because they buy themselves a sailing boat or yacht as soon as they arrive), are leaving because apartheid in South Africa is falling apart. Twenty percent of these people are going to the United States and thirty percent to the United Kingdom. Because of the much greater population there, their impact in these countries will be minimised. But fifty percent of them are coming here! In our small population of sixteen million we can expect them to be very influential, by their sheer numbers alone, but more so because they are transferring their wealth here which is why the government approves their entry.

We have long known that Australia—the last continent 'discovered' by the whites—would also be their last stronghold—the last bastion of white supremacy in the world. I know we've been saying that for a while, but now is the time to prepare for it.

I'm not a doomsday person, so let me tell you what I see. South Africa is bound to fall—it's only a matter of time. The resistance of the United States and Britain to impose economic boycotts or take other action to hasten the process is deplorable—but in another way it's a very positive step for us. The involvement of American blacks in this issue—their protests, their flexing of economic muscle—is really the first time they have, in any numbers, involved themselves in anything outside their own immediate concern. And the process by which they can and are forcing their government to heed their call is a learning process for them.

Likewise Africa. It's a long time since we have seen a united Africa. In fact, most African countries have been bogged down in their local problems, similar to the blacks in America. The problems which beleaguer African states have been made for them—by the process of colonisation. They are now maintained for them by the economic colonisation. The same can be said about blacks in the United States and elsewhere. No one is suffering from problems of their own making.

So I am forecasting the deeper recognition by blacks of a common enemy— at the same time as these potential black giants are realising their strength.

President Mugabe has implied that black Commonwealth countries are now going to apply pressure on Britain—by threatening to impose economic sanctions against Britain if she fails to apply economic sanctions against South Africa. Such a threat would devastate Britain. That sort of threat, that sort of unity, would change the entire nature of the Commonwealth relationship. Whatever happens, the awareness of the power of the black nations will have been realised.

After the fall of South Africa we'll have a different world. We'll have a world in which blacks have some small recognition of their own power and strength. However, I am talking now about those blacks over there—in the United States and in Africa. Because, here it will be a very different story.

With the influx of South Africans—not that white Australians even need their help—we'll have the 'same old story', except that it will get worse. It will get worse because the opposition to change, opposition to progress, will be greater. White elitism will be digging in its heels here. Racism will be rampant here, and we will still be here—black targets of their hostility.

No, this isn't doomsday stuff. At the same time—if we play our cards right, blacks all over the world will be realising that when the whites stole a black continent they stole it from the black world! We, as the writers, must help them to realise that.

We are the caretakers of this continent, but we too have to come to our own understanding of the nature of the world, and of our place in it. We have to understand that even if the genocide attempt made here had been successful—and we have to admit it damn near has been successful—and if we had been wiped out altogether—this country, this land, this continent would still have to be regarded as being a black continent. The minute period of time in which whites have occupied this black continent—two hundred years out of more than fifty thousand—counts for very little, and it may even count for nothing! We believed we were caretakers, and that belief is part of our heritage. It is essential that we should believe it again.

I am reminded of a saying of the native Americans, which is very relevant here. They say: 'God gave every race and colour a country. If He came back tomorrow, would you be in yours?'

That question scares folks, and they would rather not deal with it. The question goes beyond colonialism, beyond legal and moral positions. It speaks to every person who professes to believe in a God. Given the mess that the world is in today, I can understand—but not condone—why people would rather not deal with that question. Rather than being a political question, it calls upon all people to grapple with their own position here, their own motivation and rationalisation, instead of hiding behind government or the events of history.

As writers, as black writers, we have many responsibilities. Yes, we are the public sound of the black community weeping—but we are also the thorn in the national conscience. As such, we are in a position of great ambivalence. We are able, by virtue of our craft, to maintain a greater visibility and a higher

profile than many of our people. Inherent in that position, we have a greater
responsibility toward our people, greater, that is, than other blacks. We
complain amongst ourselves about the heavy weight of our communities'
expectations, and we wonder 'Why me? Why do they always expect more
of me?' But the answer is quite simple. We do have a greater responsibility,
and it is the community's interactive responsibility to call our attention to
that task, and to demand of us an answerability which goes beyond the norm.
It is their duty to demand, and it is our duty to respond.

Black writers—rather than our lives getting easier as we get the odd foot
through the door—black writers' lives will get harder. In a global sense, we
have to think through all the issues, and report on them to our communities—
and to anyone else who will listen. We have a unique vantage point in that,
in our analysis of the issues, we can also catch glimpses of the future. Now,
if we are smart and use our heads, we can use this vantage point to the
community's best advantage.

You may think that white writers also have that vantage point, but very
few have. They don't—because they've been trained by their socialisation
process as well as the milieu in which they work to watch only what the
white folks are doing. That's why the white community is always so surprised
by events. They were surprised that when they promoted Andrew Young
to be the US representative to the United Nations, he had his own agenda,
a black agenda. They were surprised when he demonstrated his access to
and status in the Arab world. It's true that he didn't go far enough—his
performance here in Australia was appalling and ignorant on the issue of
blacks, but I suppose we can't expect all things of one person. Whites were
always surprised when the Vietcong let black soldiers go free when they
were captured. They were surprised when Harold Washington ran for Mayor
of Chicago—and they were surprised when he won. They were surprised
when Jesse Jackson ran for President. They can't anticipate a healthy and
prosperous future for blacks, and so they can't predict events of a positive
nature when they involve blacks. They can't because they don't have the
means to do so.

It is therefore important that black writers not only relate the news of
the black community, and seize control of the projection of our own image—
but that we also anticipate and project our vision of the future. In the past,
control of our image has been outside of our own community, which is how
such negative stereotypes have been developed about us. When Roberta Flack
came to this country in 1973, her white tour organisers told her that we
were 'savages'. It is to her personal credit that she refused to accept this
description of us, that she came into our community and performed a free
concert in Redfern. She told us that when she was told of our savage ways,
it reminded her of what they used to say about black Americans, and what
they used to say about Africans, and that was the only reason she rejected
the description. She said that she was unable to find, in 1973, anything
concrete on which to reject their description of us—because our image at

that time was tightly controlled by whites. Many of you will remember our image back then—it was only fourteen years ago.

We've come a little way since then—but we delude ourselves if we think we've come a long way. We're writers, and playwrights and poets, but are any of us in control of making sure that what we write is published? Or are we still at the mercy of the white editor? Is our work still picked over and 'approved' by whites before it sees the light of day? Can any play get off the ground unless it is approved and funded by the white administration?

Some of us have developed our little tricks, thinking we are tricking the man. We negotiate that they won't change a word without consultation, and that sort of thing. But actually it is we who are being tricked, because by the time we are in a position to negotiate—are sufficiently recognised as writers so that we can negotiate—we have already internalised a very clear idea of what they will and will not accept. Unconsciously, perhaps, we censor our own work. We know to a 't' how much rage they will accept, how much anger, how long they will tolerate a litany on our pain, and we tailor our work around it. We may not do it deliberately, but we do it! This isn't a criticism—it's just a fact. If we are gathered at this conference to get the most out of our time, we have to look at ourselves honestly, look at our position honestly, so that we can work out what we need, and how we are going to get it. If we don't admit that control of our craft, and control of our image, still lies outside our community, then we can't talk about the means to pursue it.

One important thing I noticed in America. Blacks over there have made a lot of progress in comparison to us. But they do not control their own image. They are much more visible than us in the media. You can see them every night on television. But in that period in which the future is developed, in that time slot for children's programmes, you never see a black carrying a briefcase! In fact, I didn't see a black carrying a briefcase in any show or in any advertising commercial. I saw them carrying footballs, basketballs, all manner of sporting equipment. I saw them carrying dishwashing liquid, Ivory soap, and deodorants—and that's a lot more than we are allowed to carry on television here. But I didn't see any of them carrying a briefcase and that says a lot. I was told that Bill Cosby sometimes carried a briefcase in the Cosby show, and that it's the highest ranking show on TV. That's nice. I didn't see it, but even if I had I just don't think that embedding one black carrying a briefcase in a comedy is what I had in mind.

Control of our own image is critical to our development. We have to plan how to seize that control, and plan what we're going to do with it. It won't be much use to us if we've internalised, amongst ourselves, the negative image of ourselves which has been reflected back to us. Unfortunately, many of us have, but there are even things we can do about that. We're writers, and we have a whole range of tools at our disposal. It's true that many facts about our history have been concealed, have been destroyed, or are withheld from us. We've been doing a lot of agonising about that. So many of us—

because we are writing in a climate of desperation—want to be historically accurate, and accurate in the contemporary. I'm suggesting that far too many of us—and I know there aren't even many of us writing—but far too many of the few there are have become overly preoccupied with non-fiction. I'd like to see some of us pick up the other tools that are available to use because in some areas, what can't be accomplished in 'fact' can be accomplished in fiction. I feel it's an area we've ignored, and an area we should explore and exploit.

I believe that at least half of the currently available, white authored, 'historical' accounts of what is termed Australian settlement and analysis of contemporary Australia, is fiction. It would be a valid exercise for us to write fiction which is half fact. Our concentration on locating and validating black heroes for our children is great, but surely it's only half the exercise. We can create heroes too.

There is even a traditional precedent for this. At Strelley Station (thirty-five miles outside of Port Hedland, in Western Australia—a very traditional area) I was shown some wonderful drawings on calendars which they were printing and distributing. In several of these drawings by an elder, there were trees which showed the trunk, branches, leaves, and the roots. When I remarked on this, I was told: 'It's okay to draw not only what you see is there—but also what you know is there'. So, let it be thus with some of our heroes. We know they are there, so let's depict them.

I'm not suggesting that we confuse fiction with fact. I'm suggesting that there is a legitimate place in fiction for blacks, and that fiction is more accessible to children. Do you recall identifying with fictional characters as a child? Were you ever Tarzan? Or Superman? Or the Phantom? I've forgotten a damned lot of the non-fiction I read as a child, but Tarzan, Superman, and the Phantom will probably conjure up heroic deeds in my mind until the day I die—and unfortunately not one of them is black.

There are many ways of going about our task, and we have to use all the means available to us if we are to project a positive future. There's a lot of validity in the possibility of nuclear holocaust, for instance, and we can't for one moment overlook that. But we also have to place our bets each way. We can't allow ourselves to be paralysed with fear. We also have to plan for ourselves a future without nuclear disaster. Nuclear holocaust aside, have you read any predictive writing about Australia in which blacks play a vibrant and vital role? No? Have you read any about the world in which blacks play a vibrant and vital role? No? I haven't either. We have to change that because it's essential for our children to have a vision of a future toward which they can grow!

We writers have to—predict, invent, create—we have to project for our children, and for ourselves, a wonderful future. We have to develop that vision based on our past, and on our present, so that our better times can be seen, felt, looming just ahead of us. It has to be so tangible that our children can reach out and, almost touch it! Because we have to train them to reach out. We have to train them to anticipate good things. We have to train them to be ready for this future!

The responsibilities that we assume when we pick up our pens is awesome. I have just skimmed the surface here because I want to leave time for your questions in this period. I wanted to share these ideas so that we can discuss them over the next few days.

To summarise, we need to spend time making an honest and frank appraisal of our position. It's true that we haven't had much time, in the historical sense, in which to make an impact with our writing. Our access to this work is just too recent. We've used a lot of that time—small though it is—and a great deal of our creative energy, conveying messages out of our community. That's good, it's both necessary and therapeutic.

But now, global events will overtake us if we don't move on. We need to examine those events, and examine how they impact on us. We need to, as a group, develop strategies, and assume responsibility for tasks, to make sure we have the whole field covered. We need to work simultaneously on our historical analysis, our contemporary analysis, and the creative development of our future. We need to bring all of our collective skills to this task. We need to analyse what steps we need to take in order to regain control of our image, and of our future. What practical things we need, what technology, from where, how, and to whom.

We need also to develop caution. Oppressed groups have a tendency to overdisclose, to develop plans and then run out and tell the man. We help them to stop us by telling them what we're going to do, and where. Finally, but perhaps most importantly, we have to foster trust and unity. I know we've been talking about trust now for a long time, but we've always talked in terms of giving it or getting it. Perhaps it's time to talk of earning trust and of respecting those who have earned it, as well as those who are trying. Trust should be the reward of hard work and honest dialogue with the community. Unity would be a natural extension of that trust.